Top Notes

Amanda Lohrey's
Vertigo
Study notes for Common Module:
Texts and Human Experiences
2019–2023 HSC

Bruce Pattinson

—— A ——
FIVE SENSES
PUBLICATION

Five Senses Education Pty Ltd
2/195 Prospect Highway
Seven Hills 2147
New South Wales
Australia

Pattinson, Bruce
Top Notes – Vertigo
ISBN 978-1-76032-218-2

CONTENTS

TOP NOTES SERIES

This series has been created to assist HSC students of English in their understanding of set texts. Top Notes are easy to read, providing analysis of issues and discussion of important ideas contained in the texts.

Particular care has been taken to ensure that students are able to examine each text in the context of the module it has been allocated to.

Each text generally includes:

- Notes on the specific module
- Plot summary
- Character analysis
- Setting
- Thematic concerns
- Language studies
- Essay questions and a modelled response
- Other textual material
- Study practice questions
- Useful quotes

We have covered the areas we feel are important for students in their study of *Texts and Human Experiences* for their Common Module. I am sure you will find these Top Notes useful in your studies of English.

Bruce Pattinson
Series Editor

COMMON MODULE: TEXTS AND HUMAN EXPERIENCES

*"It is quite possible—overwhelmingly probable, one might guess—
that we will always learn more about human life and personality
from novels than from scientific psychology"*

NOAM CHOMSKY

What is the Common Module?

The Common Module set for the 2019–23 HSC is *Texts and Human Experiences*. It is compulsory to study this topic as prescribed by NESA and it is common to all three English courses. Remember: you will be learning how texts reveal individual and collective human experiences. There are no right or wrong answers in this module – it is about how you see and interpret material and engage with it.

In the Common Module you will be analysing one prescribed text and a range of short texts that are related to the idea of human experiences. You will analyse texts not only to investigate the ideas they present about this area but also how they convey these ideas. This means you will be looking closely at the techniques a composer uses to represent his / her messages and shape meaning. You will also be looking at relationships between texts in regard to the experiences you explore. Overall, you will become an expert on texts and the human experience — that is, the different notions people have about human experience and the various ways composers manipulate techniques to communicate their ideas about it.

Specifically you will look at one set text from the following list.

- Doerr, Anthony, *All the Light We Cannot See*
- Lohrey, Amanda, *Vertigo*
- Orwell, George, *Nineteen Eighty-Four*
- Parrett, Favel, *Past the Shallows*
- Dobson, Rosemary 'Young Girl at a Window', 'Over the Hill', 'Summer's End', 'The Conversation', 'Cock Crow', 'Amy Caroline', 'Canberra Morning'
- Slessor, Kenneth 'Wild Grapes', 'Gulliver', 'Out of Time', 'Vesper-Song of the Reverend Samuel Marsden', 'William Street', 'Beach Burial'
- Harrison, Jane, *Rainbow's End*
- Miller, Arthur, *The Crucible*
- Shakespeare, William, *The Merchant of Venice*
- Winton, Tim, *The Boy Behind the Curtain* Chapters: 'Havoc: A Life in Accidents', 'Betsy', 'Twice on Sundays', 'The Wait and the Flow', 'In the Shadow of the Hospital', 'The Demon Shark', 'Barefoot in the Temple of Art'
- Yousafzai, Malala & Lamb, Christina, *I am Malala*
- Daldry, Stephen, *Billy Elliot*
- O'Mahoney, Ivan, *Go Back to Where You Came From* – Series 1, Episodes 1, 2 and 3 and *The Response*
- Walker, Lucy, *Waste Land*

NESA has mandated that students must study a related text as part of the common module, and that this should be part of their in-school assessment. However there is NO LONGER a requirement to write about a related text in the HSC examination itself.

WHAT DOES NESA REQUIRE FOR THE COMMON MODULE?

The NESA documentation of the Common Module: Texts and Human Experiences states that students:

- deepen their understanding of how texts represent individual and collective human experiences;

- examine how texts represent human qualities and emotions associated with, or arising from, these experiences;

- appreciate, explore, interpret, analyse and evaluate the ways language is used to shape these representations in a range of texts in a variety of forms, modes and media;

- explore how texts may give insight into the anomalies, paradoxes and inconsistencies in human behaviour and motivations, inviting the responder to see the world differently, to challenge assumptions, ignite new ideas or reflect personally;

- may also consider the role of storytelling throughout time to express and reflect particular lives and cultures;

- by responding to a range of texts, further develop skills and confidence using various literary devices, language concepts, modes and media to formulate a considered response to texts;

- study one prescribed text and a range of short texts that provide rich opportunities to further explore representations of human experiences illuminated in texts;

- make increasingly informed judgements about how aspects of these texts, for example, context, purpose, structure, stylistic and grammatical features, and form shape meaning;

- select one related text and draw from personal experience to make connections between themselves, the world of the text and their wider world;

- by responding and composing throughout the module, further develop a repertoire of skills in comprehending, interpreting and analysing complex texts;

- examine how different modes and media use visual, verbal and/or digital language elements;

- communicate ideas using figurative language to express universal themes and evaluative language to make informed judgements about texts;

- further develop skills in using metalanguage, correct grammar and syntax to analyse language and express a personal perspective about a text

If this is what is required by NESA, we need to examine the concept of human experience carefully so we can adequately respond in these ways. I would recommend that you read the complete document which is on the NESA web site and can be downloaded in Word or Adobe. Understanding this document is an important step in handling the textual material within the guidelines required — remember you are reading for a purpose and should make notes and highlight ideas as you read so that you can develop these ideas later.

UNDERSTANDING THE COMMON MODULE

What are Human Experiences?

The concept of Human Experiences is at the heart of the Common Module.

Human Experiences are experiences of individuals or a group of people (eg a family, society, or nation) in life. There are a very wide range of human experiences which include but go beyond this list:

- feelings or reactions (momentary or long term): love, hate, anger, joy, fear, disgust
- key milestones or stages: birth, childhood, adulthood, marriage, divorce, death
- culture, belonging and identity
- conformity and rebellion
- innocence and guilt, justice
- freedom and repression
- education, vocation, work, sport, leisure
- attraction to a person, idea, group or cause
- opposition to an idea, cause, political system
- religious faith or belief
- extreme events such as an earthquake, avalanche, tsuanami
- regular events such as walking, eating, singing, dancing, discussing ideas.

The word *experience* seems innately connected to the human condition and it is something we have each day whether a mundane experience that is repetitive, or something new and dramatic which offers challenges and rewards. Experiences can vary greatly in their impact on individuals, groups and countries. One example might be a war that is a negative experience for a whole population while we may experience the wonder of medicine with a new vaccine for a deadly disease that saves millions of people. We need to note that the module asks for 'experiences' ...we are a combination of different experiences and each has a varying impact. One person's problem is another's challenge depending on perspective, skill set, previous experience and ability.

Experiences are widespread and often shared: this is why people tell their stories and these shared experiences form part of our cultural heritage. These experiences often inform, warn and teach across entire cultural groups and many stories are shared across cultures.

DEFINING HUMAN EXPERIENCES

Now let's attempt to define what human experiences are and shape them into a more coherent and easily understood framework so we can begin our investigation at a basic level of understanding before moving into more complex analysis and looking at how the texts illuminate our understanding of the term.

> *Dictionary.com* defines the term **experience** as:
>
> **noun**
> 1. a particular instance of personally encountering or undergoing something:
> 2. the process or fact of personally observing, encountering, or undergoing something:
> 3. the observing, encountering, or undergoing of things generally as they occur in the course of time:
>   *to learn from experience; the range of human experience.*
> 4. knowledge or practical wisdom gained from what one has observed, encountered, or undergone, e.g. *a man of experience.*
> 5. *Philosophy.* the totality of the cognitions given by perception; all that is perceived, understood, and remembered.
>
> **verb**
> (used with object), **experienced, experiencing.**
> 6. to have experience of; meet with; undergo; feel, e.g. *to experience nausea.*
> 7. to learn by experience.
>
> **idiom**
> 8. **experience religion**, to undergo a spiritual conversion by which one gains or regains faith in God.

Obviously there are a number of definitions according to context, but all are applicable to our study in some shape or form, as the range of human experience is so vast. The search for 'new experience' has driven much of the development of people, groups, cultures and nations over past millennia. New experiences are always met with excitement and often trepidation as to what change they might bring.

Think historically about how people have reacted to change. It can cause great upheavals in society, with violent reactions while other changes brought through various experiences are welcomed and may change how people live and comprehend the world. Experiences affect us emotionally in many cases rather than logically and when we respond emotionally, behaviours become unpredictable. This causes the paradoxes, anomalies and inconsistencies mentioned in the rubric. If we were logical beings the world would be an easier place, but probably more boring.

These definitions all point to the fact that memory is the key to experience. The experience is stored in memory and drawn upon when the circumstances are repeated or closely mimicked so we can deal with them — hopefully better than on the initial experience.

Experiences can come in many ways and the synonyms listed below for experience help us to understand the concept even further. They assist in defining how an experience can arise:

Synonyms

actions

background

contacts

involvement

know-how

maturity

participation

patience

practice

reality

sense

skill

struggle

training

understanding

wisdom

acquaintances

actuality

caution

combat

doings

empiricism

evidence

existences

exposures

familiarity

intimacy

inwardness

judgment

observation

perspicacity

practicality

proofs

savoir-faire

seasonings

sophistication

strife

trials

worldliness

forebearance

http://www.thesaurus.com/browse/experience?s=t

These synonyms show partly the vast array of words that our language has created around this concept, and also shows how important it is in the human psyche. We, as humans, want to experience. Now we will look at some examples of experiences and examine how they can have an impact. It is also important to remember that experiences do not have to be positive. You might experience a huge problem, a bereavement, a car accident, an unwelcome relationship or something totally bizarre that rocks your world. There can be a more opaque side to any experience that may need to be addressed.

The whole aim of this Common Module is to examine the text closely but also relate it to the concept of human experiences and decide how examining it in this way enables us to better understand both the text and the concept of humanity.

It is important that you unpack what each text you study shows you about human experiences and what ideas / themes arise from those experiences. Formulate your own ideas about the text.

Read the NESA Stage 6 document called *English Stage 6: Annotations of selected texts prescribed for the Higher School Certificate 2019-23* (see *www.educationstandards.nsw.edu.au*) for the set text you are studying. This document offers insights into the way each particular text should be examined by outlining key ideas and areas for clarification.

Human experiences and ways of experiencing vary due to individual circumstance and these experiences can change many things about individual lives, communities and the world. When we examine the concept of human experience in relation to a text, we need to examine the assumptions or biases we bring to it as well as how experiencing the text itself may change us and how we view things. The text may challenge and confront how we view the human experience or we may have preconceived ideas that make it more difficult for this to happen.

Students can also think about their own 'personal experience to make connections between themselves, the world of the text and their wider world.' Examining and enjoying any text is an experience in itself but it is what we take away from the text and apply that is the crucial aspect. That is not to say that every text will be enjoyed or offer a human experience that is significant either positively or negatively. Some texts may not personally engage you and that is fine. This is especially so when you begin to look for other related material that links to *Texts and Human Experiences*. We recommend that you find examples of texts that link but also personally appeal to you so that you can relate empathetically with them.

Individual Human Experiences

The idea of personal experiences is a popular and pervasive concept, especially in the literature of many cultures. Recording personal experiences as a means of sharing wisdom or more mundane daily tasks is part of human nature and we record and relate these experiences frequently. Experiences are recorded and relayed in many ways. We tell oral stories in both anecdotal and formal ways, we write, draw, sing and photograph our way into history (or not). Look at the proliferation of social media in this current century as people record their daily, even hourly, experiences for all to see. We record the most trivial details of our lives for likes and followers while the real world passes us by. Human experiences affect us on a daily basis and some experiences influence our lives and the way we live them.

Individuals seek out experiences in a variety of ways. Some seek more and more extreme experiences to test themselves against the world. Others limit their experiences. A lot of people prefer the familiar and don't actively seek new experiences. Individuals, it must be remembered, also see experiences in different ways and the same experience may have a very different impact on individuals. The one thing we can be certain about is that experiences are part of humanity and even the most limited of us have them. Many of these experiences also come from interaction with others and as noted we also like to share these experiences.

Experiences are what define us in many ways and are what makes us human.

We are going to look at four specific ways that experiences can influence us as people over the next few pages. These are physical, psychological, emotional and intellectual experiences and many experiences are a combination of these.

Physical Experience

The concept of a physical experience is tied into the human experience and part of the collective experience as well. Individuals seek physical experiences to test themselves against nature and other individuals often as part of trials and rituals, for example being integrated into a community. In modern times individuals have sought to test themselves with extreme sports and explorations into the harshest conditions and even space. Physical experiences can also change the way we see the world and others because of the chemical changes these experiences have on our bodies and mind. Physical experiences are often challenges and part of the experience is overcoming adversity. These physical challenges are often celebrated, as in the case of sports, but can also offer challenges if the experience is a negative one such as an accident or disease. Physical experiences are also often quite public and thus have permeated our societies in both their execution and how they are perceived. These physical experiences, even if experienced vicariously, have become popular across cultures and celebrated. Think of examples for yourself but most competitive sports offer examples.

Bruce Lee extends the concept of the physical experience into all aspects of life and that's what we will look at next in our analysis of human experiences –

'If you always put limits on everything you do, physical or anything else, it will spread into your work and into your life. There are no limits. There are only plateaus, and you must not stay there, you must go beyond them.'

Psychological Experience

The idea of a psychological experience is tied into many of the abstract ideas that people experience and can lead to a discussion of what is normal psychology. From the earliest times humans have attempted to alter their psychology through a number of experiences. On a simple level this can be a drug that changes the person's or group's perspective on reality. Examples of this might be alcohol or marijuana but cultural groups also use various substances to share group experiences. This can be seen in Native American cultures with *peyote*. In more modern times prescription drugs that are mood altering have been used to minimise the symptoms of psychiatric illnesses such as depression, and these mood altering drugs are common and legal. Others attempt to alter their psychology by seeing specialists in this area while others act out their condition leading to social and criminal issues. When discussing the human experience, psychology is a key issue and will form a part of most studies of experience. When taken too far this search for a new psychological experience can be harmful eg. an addiction.

Carl Jung, the famous psychologist, comments on the problems of addiction for human experiences, stating clearly that excess can be an issue:

"Every form of addiction is bad, no matter whether the narcotic be alcohol, morphine or idealism."

Emotional Experience

According to the psychologist, Robert Plutchik, there are eight basic emotions:

- **Fear** — feeling afraid.
- **Anger** — feeling angry. A stronger word for anger is rage.
- **Sadness** — feeling sad. Other words are sorrow, grief (a stronger feeling, for example when someone has died) or **depression** (feeling sad for a long time without any external cause). Some people think depression is a different emotion.
- **Joy** — feeling happy. Other words are happiness, gladness.
- **Disgust** — feeling something is wrong or nasty
- **Trust** — a positive emotion; admiration is stronger; **acceptance** is weaker
- **Anticipation** — in the sense of looking forward positively to something which is going to happen. **Expectation** is more neutral; **dread** is more negative.

https://simple.wikipedia.org/wiki/List_of_emotions

Emotions are the strongest drivers of human experience and form lasting aspects of any experience. Think about breaking up with someone you love and the emotions that drive behaviours in this situation. People have all sorts of extreme behaviours under the influence of emotions and these experiences are often the ones recorded and those which influence us most. Think about the role emotions play in our lives and the range of emotions from the list above. Consider how much emotions affect our life experiences, how they influence our decisions which decide our experiences and on a higher level consider how they affect the decisions which may seriously impact our experiences, such as politicians going to war.

Intellectual Experience

The concept of an intellectual experience is linked to decisions and experiences we have based on analysis and logic rather than the emotional choices referred to in the previous section. These intellectual experiences have changed the way we live and how we have seen our world. These experiences have affected the way we as humans have altered our world to suit our needs and lead to all the great advances in human society and thus experiences. Changes in our ideas, beliefs etc. alter the way we interact with the world and often these intellectual changes come at great cost.

Think of the time in Europe when the Church dominated and stopped scientific advances by calling them heresy/witchcraft. Open societies are more open to new ideas and this is what has hastened the pace of intellectual experiences as dominant ideologies fall away. Intellectual advances may not have the excitement that the other types produce but perhaps they have a more lasting impact on people, societies and the world in general. Ideas are powerful experiences and people hold beliefs strongly.

Immanuel Kant stated that:

> *"experience without theory is blind, but theory without experience is mere intellectual play."*

Consider this statement in the light of what we have learnt about human experiences. Are they a combination of many factors or can we isolate experiences into simple forms?

What exactly is a human experience?

The titular question reminds us of the old brainteaser: "If a tree falls in a forest and no one is around to hear it, does it make a sound?"

There are two classic responses to this. The more Platonically-minded would say the tree always makes a sound when it falls in the forest. We don't have to be there to hear it; we can imagine the sound of a tree falling in the forest, based on memory of such an event or on the recording of such an event. We know that sound is just vibrating air, and it's safe to say that air always vibrates in response to a tree falling, or a bear growling, or a cicada singing, whether we are there to hear it or not.

The second answer is a more post-structuralist response: the sound doesn't occur on its own; it needs a human ear to be heard. Therefore, if there is no human in the forest to hear the tree fall, then there is no sound. This automatically implies that "experience" of anything requires the presence of a human being, which means there is no such thing as an experience that *isn't* human.

Animal rights activists – or anyone with a beloved pet – would almost certainly reject this notion because it prioritises humans and relegates all other species to a lower class of being: an attitude that most would agree has gotten the human race into an awful lot of environmental trouble over the last 200 years of industrialisation.

In his article (*What is an Experience?*), my learned colleague Paul Hartley describes experience in its most basic form, as "the perception of something else" and "ultimately information about what we have perceived." But does this make it particularly human? Dogs and cats perceive things. Insects perceive things. You could even say that plants perceive things, such as the direction from which the sun is shining. Perception is the most basic of life's survival tools for all manner of flora and fauna.

In her brief but cogent disquisition on the subject (*What is Human?*), another of my learned colleagues, Nadine Hare, asserts that to be human is a social construct. Hartley builds on that notion by suggesting that culture affects experience when we start to share it, because "the words, associations, and priorities we attach to the shared experience define how we understand the world we live in."

Hare rightly points out that this world is increasingly dominated by consumerism, which has distorted what it means to be human by excluding all of the attributes and qualities that "make people people." Calling us consumers reduces our experiences to mere transactions. It defines human experience within the narrow confines of the purchase funnel and has little interest in anything that isn't a purchase driver.

Perhaps the field of commerce is where the experiential rubber most emphatically meets the road. Unlike mere perception, commerce is a uniquely human experience. It has mediated, automated, and dominated the human agenda to the point where we are defined by what we buy and little else. Commerce has invaded the non-profit spheres of government, health, and education, imposing its own priorities and principles on these institutions in the expectation that they will behave more like businesses. And even though business still strives to appeal to the so-called masses, it prioritises the pursuit of individual wealth, and in so doing, not only inhibits the desire for shared experience but unravels the social fabric historically woven by the democratic tradition.

As if in response, that social fabric is being re-woven by our networks. As Hare asserts, "humans both produce technology and are produced through technology." Experience is shared more now than it ever has been because the experiential platform – i.e., that very human invention called the internet – is in place to facilitate it like never before, and on a global scale.

This sharing capability reintroduces all of those things that "make people people" back into the conversation – whether commercial or political. What "makes people people" is messy, unpredictable, emotional, and complex. Most of what makes us human has no place in the experiential confines of the purchase funnel, and defies any of our attempts to place it there.

The challenge for us as a species is to embrace this new capacity for sharing to keep the agendas of our hegemonic institutions – whether commercial or political – from defining what makes an experience human. A post-consumer business strategy might be one that, as Hare hopes, will "expand our view of people to include the complex and dynamic social, cultural, gendered, spiritual and racialised beings that they are." Maybe then will our shared human experience truly become, as Hartley asserts, the glue that holds us all together as human beings.

Will Novosedlik
MISC magazine

https://miscmagazine.com/what-is-a-human-experience/

This article appeared in the September 2014 edition of MISC magazine. Can you relate to what the article says about human experiences? Do human experiences depend on perception? Does the experience of anything require the presence of a human as experiencer (para 3)? Can the ideas of experience be extended to include perception by plants or animals? Hartley's idea is that "shared human experience" is "the glue that holds us all together as human beings". Is this an oversimplification?

The Impact of Human Experiences

Human experiences have impacts on many levels. On an individual level, we can have changes in our assumptions about the world and people around us; we can ingest new ideas and have these open new vistas of productivity and performance. We can also reflect and build on these experiences to ensure that they are even more meaningful to our lives. Behaviours towards others and the way we respond to the world can manifest themselves in new and different responses. An example might be that through adverse experiences we can build resilience so that the next negative experience isn't as traumatic and we accept it for what it is. Experiences also teach us new behaviours on a very physical level — if you burn yourself once on a flame you learn not to do it again (hopefully).

The impact of human experiences can also be shared in groups and societies. Firstly, let's examine some group dynamics that can be affected by human experiences. Groups share experiences and adapt and develop behaviours that impact on the group as a whole. Think about the notorious 'bonding' sessions sporting teams have that unite them in a common goal. Think about the behaviours of various gangs in our society. We see plenty of examples of this on American television where gangs based on ethnicity and social groupings form specific sets of behaviours that impact on how they interact with each other and the world. These groupings carry assumptions about how they see the world and respond to it. For example, they may have generally negative reactions to law enforcement and this is ingrained into their codes of behaviour. They are suspicious of the world and the people in it — dividing them up into threats, the law and victims. These behaviours are often reinforced by group experiences such as the initiation rituals which are integral to membership.

Often the impact of these behaviours is to perpetuate stereotypes that then categorise the individuals within these groups. The graphic I have included here shows a stereotypical gang member with the suspicious gaze, ubiquitous hoody and scruffy look. These stereotypes reject new ideas and maintain assumptions about the world, often to the detriment of their members. The experiences they have reinforce their own stereotypical way of viewing anything outside the safety of the group and the cycle continues. Of course, other groups have more positive impacts and see the world as a  very different place and their experiences are designed to be positive interactions. Think about groups such as Rotary who are constructive in the community. Other groups have specialty interests such as Animal Welfare, Surf Lifesaving and charities.

Normal social interactions impact groups and individuals, but it takes a major event to alter the behaviours of whole societies, especially so in the modern world where societies are large in scale. Earlier in human history smaller experiences could alter the behaviour of societies as they were insignificant in size compared to modern ones. We often fail to remember that many of these ancient societies' behaviours were impacted by superstition, religions and cultural habituation. The modern society as we know it is only a recent phenomenon. Just a few hundred years ago with church rule people were forced to think in a specific

way and punished for not adhering to a theological culture. Think of the Spanish Inquisition, the imprisonment of Galileo and other such restrictions on freedom of thought; scientific breakthroughs were hidden or declared witchcraft. Even recently the world has seen societies kept repressed by failed ideologies. The brutality of such regimes has left deep scars on the social psyche of nations as they try to recover. This has had an impact on the human experiences of whole populations, and societies respond accordingly.

One example might be at the conclusion of the Communist regime in East Germany when the Berlin Wall was destroyed as a visual symbol of the new-found freedom of a whole population of people who had been repressed for decades by a brutal and ever-present regime. Many citizens who had grown up in this system, where you could 'disappear' without trial or real evidence, found the idea that you could express yourself incredible. Many of the

East Germans couldn't believe that this freedom was real and that the Stasi (the secret police) were gone.

Other experiences can affect societies in extreme ways. Think about wars and the impact they have on civilian populations.

Climatic events such as earthquakes change the way that people behave and respond to situations. Catastrophic flooding occurred in the US city of New Orleans in 2005. The US President's response to help was not immediate and the national administration was severely criticised for lack of effective action.

Societies also respond to perceived problems such as pollution. In 1989 the oil tanker Exxon Valdez ran aground in Prince William Sound, Alaska with disastrous results. The effects of this event are still being experienced thirty years later.

Societies can be divided, as we saw with the election of Donald Trump in the United States of America and the reaction of the Political Left.

The impact of human experiences on societies can be quite dramatic, as we have seen, while other experiences (such as an election) can go by without a murmur from societies, no matter who wins. As a last thought before we move on you should also consider the impact of the media on societies in the modern world, and how they influence individuals, societies and the development of ideas.

Problems With Human Behaviour

So far, we have discussed the impact of human experiences on behaviour. Now we can begin to develop some more complex judgements and understandings about the impact of those experiences on human behaviours. In simplistic terms it could be assessed as:

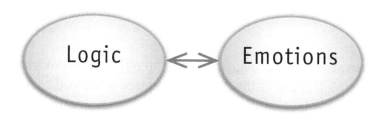

These two opposites on the continuum certainly shape the manner in which we see incidents and how they affect the experience. For instance, if someone you love has no interest in you, it creates a very different reaction to someone you don't care about having no interest in you. It is generally agreed that humans respond more strongly with emotion than they do with logic. Often, it is only through time and reflection that we can understand how an experience has changed and/or altered the manner in which we see a situation or individual.

The Role of Storytelling in Human Experiences

Storytelling has been part of the human experience since 'people' began communicating and it is a method used to convey information and experience as well as be entertaining. Earliest myths were all oral and then people began to write down stories so they weren't lost in time. From this, various theories have developed around storytelling and one is the 'monomyth', which is a template across cultures for storytelling. Let's have a look at this below.

'In narratology and comparative mythology, the monomyth, or the hero's journey, is the common template of a broad category of tales that involve a hero who goes on an adventure, and in a decisive crisis wins a victory, and then comes home changed or transformed.

The concept was introduced in *The Hero with a Thousand Faces* (1949) by Joseph Campbell, who described the basic narrative pattern as follows:

> "A hero ventures forth from the world of common day into a region of supernatural wonder: fabulous forces are there encountered and a decisive victory is won: the hero comes back from this mysterious adventure with the power to bestow boons on his fellow man."

Campbell and other scholars, such as Erich Neumann, describe narratives of Gautama Buddha, Moses, and Christ in terms of the monomyth. Critics argue that the concept is too broad or general to be of much use in comparative mythology. Others say that the hero's journey is only a part of the monomyth; the other part is a sort of different form, or colour, of the hero's journey.

Storytelling in History and its Purpose in Human Experience

Storytelling in oral form was accompanied by some theatrics to make the stories as entertaining as possible. Many of the early narratives were based upon religious ceremonies and stories of the creation of the earth and people(s). As time moved on, these stories were accompanied by dance, music and/or theatre and often were part of lengthy rituals, often taking days. These stories were designed to bring meaning to people's lives by explaining their own existence and the purpose/meaning of life in a time when life expectancy was short and entertainment was scarce. Of course stories were also recorded as these experiences were significant to all people and these stories run across all cultures. Before writing, stories were recorded in pictures such as cave art, in tattoo designs on skin and in designs such as rock piles and the giant carved heads of Easter Island.

Writing changed the manner in which stories were told and many of the old oral traditions were lost, barely being kept alive by specialists. Stories began to travel across cultural and national boundaries on whatever surface could be created. Papyrus, bones, pottery, skins, paper and in more modern times film, video and digital storage have changed, over time, the way in which stories of human experience have been told and shared. Content evolved from myth, fable and legend to history, personal narratives and commentary. Modern narrative form often has an educational or didactic element and can drift into propaganda. Stories of self-revelation can be instructive and give audiences the opportunity to apply learning to individual lives, whereas historically narrative was used in this way for societies and groups as a whole. In recent times narratives have become interactive and audiences can choose how the narrative unfolds.

Whatever form the story takes we all have a seemingly innate need for narratives to make sense of our lives. They either confirm our world view or alter our world view depending on the experience they convey and the experiences that we bring to the narrative. We need to remember that narratives are important to human experience and have been significant since the beginning of time.

The Text as an Experience

The concept of the text as an experience is one area to consider as we look at *Texts and Human Experiences*. Reading or viewing the text is an experience in itself and when we do this we bring our own history (experiences) to the text and this helps shape our understanding.

Think about the personal perspective that you bring to a text. What are some of your experiences that might influence how you read a particular text? Some texts, especially personal narratives of trial and tribulation or loss, can be confronting to some audiences and bring back strong opinions or emotions. Many texts attempt to do this as they convey a particular point of view about the world.

Does what you bring to the text affect what you learn from that text? We also need to delve into how the narrative experience is conveyed and how this in turn impacts upon the manner in which the story is received by audiences across different cultures. For example, Western films where heroes fight Islamic terrorism may well be viewed very differently by audiences in Western democracies and Islamic countries. Even seemingly innocuous narratives like the movie 'The Red Pill' which is about men's rights and created by a woman, has caused a polarisation of views wherever it has been shown. Strong personal experiences and viewpoints certainly bring their own understandings to texts.

Questions for Texts and Human Experiences

- Define the module in your own words.
- How are people connected by shared experiences?
- How might physical experience(s) change the way you respond to the world?
- How do you think a person's context and prior experiences shape how they perceive the world?
- Are experiences unique or do prior experiences have an impact on a current experience and way of seeing life?
- What is positive about human experiences?
- Discuss what is negative about human experiences.
- To what extent does experience shape the way we see other people and/or groups?
- Is an individual's culture part of their experience or is it something else?
- Is it possible not to have any meaningful experiences at all?
- Why do people tell stories?
- What do you think you might learn from a narrative?

STUDYING A FICTION TEXT

The medium of any text is very important. If a text is a novel this must not be forgotten. Novels are *read*. This means you should refer to the "reader" but the "responder" can also be used when you are referring to the audience of the text.

The marker will want to know you are aware of the text as a novel and that you have considered its effect as a written text.

Remembering a fiction text is a written text also means when you are exploring *how* the composer represents his/her ideas you MUST discuss language techniques. This applies to any response you do using a novel, irrespective of the form the response is required to be in.

Language techniques are all the devices the author uses to represent his or her ideas. They are the elements of a fiction that are manipulated by authors to make any novel represent its ideas effectively! You might also see them referred to as stylistic devices or narrative techniques.

Every fiction uses language techniques differently. Some authors have their own favourite techniques that they are known for. Others use a variety to make their text achieve its purpose.

Some common language techniques are shown on the diagram that follows.

LANGUAGE TECHNIQUES

Setting – *where does the action take place? Why? Does the setting have symbolic meaning?*

Main Character portrayal/development: *How does the character develop? What is the reader to learn from this?*

Minor Character use: *How does the author use the minor characters to represent ideas about themes or major characters?*

Narrative Person: *what is the effect this has on the narrative and the reader's response to it?*

LANGUAGE TECHNIQUES

Humour

Symbols and motifs: *how is repetition of image/idea used to maximise the novel's effect?*

Images: *similes, metaphors, personification*

Tone: *not just of character comments but also of the narration*

Conflict: *the action, Man vs man, Man vs nature, and/or Man vs himself*

Aural techniques: *Alliteration, assonance and onomatopoeia, rhythm*

Dialogue: *not just what is said but how is important to idea representation*

THE AUTHOR

"I'm trying to capture a sense of the numinous, a sense of being a small part of a great whole, that wonderful feeling that has nothing to do with God or religion."

Amanda Frances Lillian Lohrey (1947 –) is an Australian author who now works out of the University of Queensland. Not just a novelist she also pens essays! Some of which may be found at *http://www.themonthly.com.au/author/amanda-lohrey* if you are interested in some more topical writing. A more comprehensive analysis of her biographical details and works can be found at the following links.

The link below is to the official site of her publisher.

http://www.blackincbooks.com/authors/amanda-lohrey

The following is a lengthy article on Lohrey written in The Australian newspaper by Geordie Williamson that discusses her work in general terms.

http://www.theaustralian.com.au/arts/review/amanda-lohrey-is-a-class-act-story-fn9n8gph-1226597132344?nk=cab4f7992d97a2c7128e24855febe807

The link below is to an Australian Broadcasting Commission site that explores her work in terms of thematic concerns and her influences.

http://www.abc.net.au/radionational/programs/bookshow/reading-madame-bovary-an-interview-with-amanda/2961178

Again the link below isn't specifically on Vertigo but it does give good background to her work and the ideas that drive her writing. Includes some discussion on techniques. From *The Age* newspaper.

http://www.theage.com.au/articles/2004/03/17/1079199287180.html?from=storyrhs

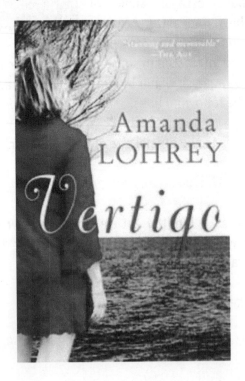

PUTTING THE NOVELLA IN CONTEXT

Vertigo is an Australian novella but deals with concerns such as love that are universal, thus it has a wider appeal. The main context therefore is understood by readers studying this text for the HSC. The two other issues that may cause some concern for readers are the concepts of seachange/ treechange which are dealt with in later sections of this study guide and bushfires which can be readily researched for those that have no experience. Most readers will have seen footage on television of bushfires and the problems they cause.

A bushfire fact sheet can be found at:

http://www.climateinstitute.org.au/articles/publications/facts-and-myths-about-bushfires-and-climate-change.html?gclid=CJDi6700t9QCFZOGKgodBh4Hcw

which looks at bushfire facts and fiction. Another site that lists the worst bushfires says of Tasmania's worst;

> 'Black Tuesday (TAS), 7 Feb 1967 - An unusually abundant spring covered Tasmanian forest floors with litter, providing excess fuel for the bushfire season. Strong northerly winds and high temperatures coupled to help fuel at least 80 different fires across southern Tasmania, which swept over the south-east coast of the state and

came within 2km of central Hobart. The fires killed 62 people and razed almost 1300 homes.'

What you need to read are the two articles below which offer a deep insight into the construction and development of Vertigo and how Lohrey conceived and perceives the novella. These two links take you to pages directly relevant to your studies and some of which I have quoted in the body of this guide. Read them carefully, they are not long, and you will have a clear insight into the text.

The first is an interview from the Age newspaper in Melbourne with Lohrey which covers her novella and its relevance and composition.

The second is an interview from Radio National which can be downloaded but I used the transcript which is accessible by clicking the relevant button on the page. It is an extensive interview on the text covering a wide range of issues. Highly recommended.

While our main focus in this instance must be the human experiences that occur in the novel, and we will certainly deal with these in the ideas section of this guide, these other contextual idea are relevant in that they frame these human experiences.

PLOT OUTLINE

Anna is introduced

Luke is introduced

Their lives are in need of change

They decide to move to the coast from the city

A house is found in Garra Nalla

Life in Garra Nalla is good for Luke who is bird-watching

Gil is their neighbour and he becomes a friend

Anna becomes unsettled and misses 'the boy'.

Anna and Luke befriend the Watts family

The first smoke from the bushfire is seen in the distance

Preparations are made around the house as the fire comes nearer

The wind continues and the town is threatened

The fire arrives and they are rescued then evacuated.

It is a cathartic moment for both as' the boy' disappears and then they seem to adjust

Luke and Anna return and find the house is fine

The township returns to some form of normalcy

Anna and Luke appear to reconcile and are ready to restart their lives.

PLOT SUMMARY

Vertigo is a novella and a pastoral (both of these terms are defined below). It is unusual in its structure as it is written in three extended sections rather than the more regular structure of chapters. Understanding these terms will enable us to get an idea of Lohrey's concept prior to engaging with the content/narrative.

Novella *(From Wikipedia, the free encyclopedia)*

- A novella is a text of written, fictional, narrative prose normally longer than a short story but shorter than a novel, somewhere between 7,500 and 40,000 words.

- The novella is generally not as formally experimental as the long story and the novel can be, and it usually lacks the subplots, the multiple points of view, and the generic adaptability that are common in the novel. It is most often concerned with personal and emotional development rather than with the larger social sphere. The novella generally retains something of the unity of impression that is a hallmark of the short story, but it also contains more highly developed characterisation and more luxuriant description.

Pastoral *(from dictionary.com)*

- *(adjective)* having the simplicity, charm, serenity, or other characteristics generally attributed to rural areas: **as in** *pastoral scenery; the pastoral life.*

- *(adjective)* pertaining to the country or to life in the country; rural; rustic.

- *(adjective)* portraying or suggesting idyllically the life of shepherds or of the country, as a work of literature, art, or music: *pastoral poetry; a pastoral symphony.*

- *(noun)* a poem, play, or the like, dealing with the life of shepherds, commonly in a conventional or artificial manner, or with simple rural life generally; a bucolic.

By considering *Vertigo* as a pastoral we may conclude that Luke and Anna are searching for an idyllic lifestyle when they leave the city behind to live in Garra Nalla. But what does this mean for our reading of the novel? In one sense it is the supposed relaxed and gentle atmosphere of the country that our two characters expect from their move. Yet it is also, in the context of our study, the images Lohrey creates to describe the supposed sleepiness of the town which makes the contrast with the fire so great. Later we will examine the symbolism of the fire but for now let us begin to explore the narrative and don't forget the impact of the graphics interwoven with the text. Think, as you read, about why they are there, how you see their effectiveness and what contribution they make to the text. You might also think if the images provided detract from the imaginative processes of the reader as we visualise the scene in our minds. All this contributes to our understanding of the experiences they have and the perception of those experiences.

I

Lohrey opens with a description of Luke Worley's newfound interest in bird watching at age thirty-four since moving to the coast with his wife, Anna. They have moved from the city where there were few birds and less pollution for Anna's asthma. With his own position under question he broaches the subject of moving to the country with Anna and she is 'receptive'. Work would go with them as they were independent in that regard and both felt a need to change with their youth fading and little hope of affording housing. Anna felt she needed something more than her current life and was in a 'spiritual impasse'.

They begin to plan their move and search for locations with some conditions. Eventually they come across Garra Nalla which is a small place of about eighty houses. Note all through this search we get the image of the 'son' who is with them. This is a recurring image and later it is revealed he is the son they lost to a miscarriage—it is like an emotional link manifested that seems entirely real to them. Garra Nalla is described in detail and is perfect for them. Later they find it has a dangerous beach and their friends say 'there's nothing here!' Yet the Federation era house which was just right, especially when they found it was affordable. Luke wasn't concerned about the perils of rural living and so they moved in and begin a new phase in their lives.

Life has slowed down for them and Anna has gifted Luke new binoculars so he can watch birds. They take much pleasure in identifying the Striated Pardalote and even more in the house which they adore, even the 'boy' loves the verandah. The couple build a garden and begin to develop a rhythm similar to the earth. The only problem is the drought which has made water a problem. Their tanks are low and some days water is the only topic. Gilbert Rielly (Gil) is their widower neighbour and he fills them in on local folklore and gossip and they also learn the idiosyncrasies of their other neighbour, Rodney Banfield, the local plumber who is having an affair and allegedly growing marijuana.

Luke begins to develop patterns of behaviour and prefers walking to swimming. He enjoys and is often mesmerised by the bird life. One day walking home he sees a bird that is entirely new to him and he is 'elated'. He can't find the bird's name in his research but he tells Anna it is like their boy, which was never named. Luke then 'sees' the boy the next morning. We then read the story of the old squatter's mansion and how the new owners do not fit into the local scene. Gil has caught them shooting at swans, a once common occurrence.

Anna purchases a canoe despite having never paddled anything before but they soon learn after a lesson from local boy, Jacob. They glide across the water and begin to spend the evenings and sometimes the 'boy' is with them. Luke begins to dream around this time, mostly about the boy. He reads at night when it's quiet while Anna trawls the cable news channels just as her father did. In the old shed out the back Luke has found two trunks full of dusty books left by the old vicar. These books are not all theology but more travel writing which Luke gives himself over too. He reads *The Land That Is Desolate* a book of journeys in Palestine and the author is very critical of the place. He stops reading and heads out to the verandah to absorb nature.

II

The couple are settling in to life in the country and they now have to contend with the drought as they are on tank water. They now have to understand the weather and Luke finds he is more 'practical' than he has ever been before. Luke and Anna develop a friendship with Alan and Bette Watts who have two children, Zack and Briony. They play tennis together and one day, after meeting the helicopter

pilots from the army base, Luke realises he is old before his time and regrets it. The topic turns to water and Alan has devised some water saving ideas and is thinking of buying a desalination plant. Anna tells Bette they have put starting a family on hold, hoping the 'boy' isn't listening.

Ken, Luke's father comes to stay and he is a 'restless' man, not yet adjusted to retirement. He thinks the place isn't suitable for a family and wonders why Luke isn't 'sick of it'. They linguistically dance around that 'other business' with Anna. Anna notices how Ken is unsettled and that the boy never appears when he or Gil are around.

Spring is now well underway and it appears to be a 'difficult' one as no rain appears and the winds are strong. It is the worst wind for many years and everything vegetative seems burnt and faded. Anna tries to maintain her routine of running and swimming but the wind, after forty-one days is getting on her nerves. Anna has her first encounter with a snake after the washing blows off the line and this, according to Gil, makes her a local. Months pass and the rains don't come and here the weather is the 'plot' not the backdrop as it is in the city. Anna writes of it to her sister in Hong Kong. It is the topic of conversation and Anna is beginning to feel trapped, unlike Luke who can avoid it as a distraction.

While Anna might consider leaving Luke won't even think about it yet. He has an overload of work which is interfering with his reading yet he manages to get to Jerusalem as he follows Sir Frederick Treves on his journey through Palestine. Treves reminds Luke of his father, rational and sceptical. Anna continues to watch the cable news and tonight we have bloodied images of the Iraqi war. Anna is content that her 'boy' will not have to be a soldier.

Alan and Luke talk about the travel books and the conversation turns to Gil's grandson in Afghanistan where he is a commando. Gil never talks about it because of superstition and Luke realises he hasn't thought about the 'boy' for a long time now. On the way home he sees a dead swan.

It is now November and the air is dry and it gets hotter each day. Even the native animals are struggling. On the verandah in the evening Anna thinks about moving back to the city while Luke watches a sea eagle fly. She broaches the subject but he continues to watch the eagle. She goes inside and Luke is aware of her every move, he just doesn't know how to respond. 'Luke Worley is not a fool' and Luke agrees to house sit for some friends in Randwick. As they leave Garra Nalla Luke looks back and knows its home. When they arrive in the city he becomes 'irritable and censorious' and leaves after five days. Anna enjoys it more and loves escaping the wind but in the second week she misses her home. She feels she doesn't belong anywhere anymore but does notice the boy is missing in the city and thinks he sides with his father. Anna decides she needs a project and buys a book on coastal plants so she can leave a legacy in Garra Nalla when she leaves. Anna decides on she-oaks to begin her garden as she loves the way they have a 'eerie whistle' in the wind.

When she arrives back home Luke and Gil are getting materials to build a snake proof fence and Gil warns her against she-oaks as they 'burn like buggery'. Anna checks on this and finds he is correct. One night Gil comes over angry that a 'consortium' is going to take over sheep land for a tree farm that will surround the community. It threatens to increase the fire risk, wreck the water table and increase chemicals in the area. Anna is upset but Luke shrugs it off and again Anna thinks the boy takes his side.

As time passes Anna begins to resent Luke, feeling that her desire for him is not enough. She thinks he has lost ambition and the sharpness he had back in the city. She thinks he wastes time with Rodney, watching birds. He returns one day from his meandering walks and she thinks him a stranger. She has 'lost her roots' and feels disorientated, perhaps because the boy has gone and 'the inner landscape of her consciousness is beginning to fade.'

III

At the end of November Anna and Luke head to the nursery with the Watts so they all can then go and have lunch at the renovated Wolga pub. This makes Anna feel better and the following Sunday they plant their saplings according to Anna's plan and then have a celebration with Gil and the Watts. When the guests leave Luke takes Anna inside to make love after which they fall asleep on the verandah. When they awake there is smoke in the air. It is a bushfire that is a long way away at that point. Alan Watts returns and says it's a 'hell of a conflagration' and Alan reassures them no bushfire has ever reached the coast.

The next morning the smoke is in the house and covers the town but they can't see any flame. Anna checks her asthma medication which she hasn't used since living here just in case. The day is a scorcher and it's impossible to keep cool. The smoke gets worse and cuts visibility until the wind comes at night. They can now see the flames which are engrossing with their 'queer beauty'.

They feel the tension now despite the distance of the fires and Anna realises she hasn't seen the boy for weeks which keeps her awake all night. At dawn she is consoled by the comfort of her kitchen before she returns to bed to sleep. Later she awakens to find Luke with tea and news the fires are at the foothills. They now need to prepare for the fire which they do by completing jobs like gutter cleaning. Anna has soot all over her by the time she is finished and then the power is cut. Now they have no pumps to defend the house.

They head to Gil's to see what's happening and he is barbecuing sausages. He says the fire has never reached the coast so they return home, have dinner and settle in for the night. Luke returns to Sir Frederick Treves travels in Palestine as the story 'haunts' him. Finally in Nazareth the author finds something that does not disappoint him, Damascus. Treves writes about it with 'lyrical descriptions' and Luke wonders how a Christian could be made 'happy' by a 'citadel of Islam'. While he reads, Anna works on her laptop writing to her sister in Hong Kong but she is content here and not jealous of her sister. Later she worries that the fire will come and wonders what they might lose. She dreams they have to leave but can't find the boy and awakens to lighter winds but Luke says things are getting worse and they are under full alert on the coast.

They listen to the radio as things worsen. Wolga and the pub have been destroyed and a second front has begun outside the town. Alan rings and they decide to play tennis to break the tension, staying by the sea rather than fleeing. As they play they see a Forestry chopper fly over and Luke notices Anna is using her puffer. They are exhausted by the heat and go home to shower and then walk to the headland to see the fire but as they can do nothing head home to wait. In the afternoon the winds come and everything turns a 'dull greyish yellow'. The winds get worse, about one hundred and forty kilometres an hour and they decide to go back to the headland despite the wind. They can see this is where the townspeople have gathered and they can see the fire coming. Around the point they can see houses being eaten by the flames and even the sandhills burn.

Later the wind changes and the fire on the sandhills begins to turn on itself. They feel safer but Luke says he'll stay to watch as he wouldn't be able to sleep anyway. Suddenly Bette sees the fire sweeping down from the north. This was unexpected... they hadn't been looking to the north because they had been watching the southern fire. The fire races toward the town and breaks across the paddocks to the 'edge of the settlement'. Some are told to head to the rocks and sea while Anna and Luke go back to fight for their home. The house is well prepared and Luke heads outside as the fire strikes suddenly. Luke rushes back to the house to get Anna inside as the 'tidal wave of flame' hits them. Now they cannot escape to the water and as Luke prepares to go outside to fight a fire truck arrives and they get in. It instantly takes off as the flames surround it and they race away as the mirror on the side of the truck begins to melt and distort with the intense heat. They make it to the lagoon under Luke's directions and the driver thinks they are very lucky.

The truck leaves and they then see many of the local people at and in the lagoon to escape the heat. Anna joins them and around her neck are her CDs in a plastic bag. The plastic has melted and she thinks how stupid of her. Luke is very concerned about her and repeats 'Are you alright?' And she replies she is. Darkness has now come but they can only hear the fire as the smoke is thick. Later

they are taken across the lagoon where the police tell them they are to be taken to a church hall for the night. They are told they cannot return home as the town is a crime scene.

At the hall they meet survivors who have fared worse than they have. Anna finds an empty mattress while Luke gets food and drink. Luke half-heartedly eats then falls asleep and Anna fondly thinks this is typical of him. She cannot sleep and looks around the hall, dozing off until pain in her shoulder wakes her. She finds the boy snuggling into her and she traces his features with her finger. She knew he was 'indestructible'.

At dawn they 'stumble' out of the hall and all they can see are charcoal remains. Only three houses in Garra Nalla have been destroyed and they wonder whose they were. They learn their home has been untouched except for a 'thin layer of ash' over everything. They find a dead bird inside, it is the bird in the banksia tree and Luke is 'distraught' to Anna's exasperation and anger. She moves to the bedroom to shower, which will make things better, when she sees his blue jumper on the bed. It has a brown scorch mark from where an ember came in through the broken pane. It didn't catch or the house may have burnt down. She wants to cry but saves it for later when Luke calls for her. He is on the verandah watching Gil rake embers. They move toward him and Luke shouts. Gil waves casually and they ask about the Watts. They are home and Gil is happy no one is dead.

They learn Garra Nalla had survived a 'perfect firestorm' and the Watts had survived by clinging to the rocks in the sea. Gil says he was terrified of losing his kids. Later that evening Luke slips away from the house and wanders through the nature reserve. It has been destroyed and he feels 'gutted'. He weeps and is back in the hospital when Anna had birthed the boy, prematurely and dead. They had never suspected and in their shock had just thought of him as 'the boy'. They had scattered his ashes at sea, wearing the jumper that had saved them in the fire. At home Anna worries about Luke and she has searched for him all over town but heads home. Here she talks disconnectedly to her mother and then cleans up. He returns late evening and she sees he has been crying. She has never seen him cry before and he says it isn't the fire and she knows it is the boy. They hold each other for a long time and that night the boy comes in a dream to her. He waves to her and dissolves and she awakens crying until she lies staring into the dark.

On the third Sunday in December the townspeople gather on a windless day to celebrate their 'deliverance'. It is important for the kids to see things are normal and as the party winds up Anna is feeling a little drunk back at the Watts'. She now thinks she might go off the pill as life is so 'unpredictable' you shouldn't hold off decisions. She looks out over the lagoon and sees a figure, the boy, heading out to a sloop, for his next destination. She now knows he is leaving them and she is good with it. Then Bette sees the swans have returned.

Luke crashes when they arrive home because of his drinking at the party and is lost in a dream about birds. Anna takes time in the bathroom but isn't sleepy so she goes into the kitchen to watch the cable news. Not all the she-oaks were burnt and she thinks back to when Luke paddled her across the lagoon with the boy nestled in her arms. The final visual is the 'ghostly images' of the television in the dark.

QUESTIONS

Section One

1. Why do you think Lohrey begins *Vertigo* with Luke and his new bird watching habit? What impression is she making about him and the way he lives? Why might he enjoy this experience?

2. Anna is introduced next and Lohrey builds a picture of her and her life. How do you see Anna after this initial reading? What is the defining experience in her life at this point?

3. What motivates the Worley's to move to Garra Nalla? Discuss how a change of scenery might impact on their perspective of life.

4. Describe Garra Nalla in your own words.

5. What is it about the house that inspires them to buy it?

6. Give three examples of how Luke changes after the move. Find an experience he has in this section of the novella that supports these ideas.

7. Why does water become an obsession for them?

8. Describe Gil and state his impact on the couple.

9. How do you feel about the continual appearance of 'the boy' in the novella? What impact on the narrative does he have as a character?

10. What happens in Luke's recurring dream?

11. Who was *A.E. Henley Esq* and what treasures has he left for Luke to find?

Section Two

1. What impact does the drought have on the Worley's? How is experiencing the drought different for them?

2. Describe the Watts family and their lifestyle.

3. What excuse does Anna give Bette for not starting a family?

4. Discuss how Ken's arrival impacts the situation at Garra Nalla. What kind of man is he? How does he see Anna's defining experience? How does she defy his assumptions about life?

5. What is 'the other business' that Ken refers to?

6. Why is the wind becoming an issue? How many days does Anna say the wind has blown?

7. How does Anna encounter the snake? Can this be considered a negative experience or something else?

8. What does Anna tell Stephanie, her sister, in the email?

9. Why does Lohrey include the sections where Luke is reading and Anna is watching the war news (p65-67)? Are these visually distinctive and contrasting images? Is this the true experience of marriage or is Lohrey making a specific comment about the couple's experience?

10. Where is Gil's son and what is he doing?

11. Discuss how they have different views of the city when they return? They see the same things but interpret them differently. Is this part of what having new experiences means? How do the couple see the city now?

12. Why is Gil opposed to the new forest development? What does he see happening to the area?

13. What is your impression of Anna at the conclusion of this section of *Vertigo*? Have her newfound experiences changed the way she sees the world and people? Have her emotional responses altered?

Section Three

1. Why does Anna create the new garden? What is she attempting to achieve here?

2. What is the first description of the bushfire (p91)? Why does it seem unthreatening?

3. Discuss how Lohrey builds tension before the arrival of the fire. Think about the different expectations people have about the fire based on previous experiences.

4. What preparations do they make for the coming fire?

5. Why is Anna so worried about the fires?

6. Consider why they play tennis with the Watts? How might this experience ease the tension?

7. Who notices the fire is coming in from the north? Why is this significant for the townspeople?

8. How does the arrival of the fire truck help Luke and Anna?

9. Where are they evacuated to and what happens there?

10. What impact has the fire had on their home and their lives?

11. How does Gil see the events of the past few days?

12. Why does Luke cry and exhibit so much emotion at this time? How does Anna see his individual experience that created this emotion?

13. Do you think the novella ends positively, neutrally or

negatively about the Worley's and their future? Explain your response with direct reference to the text. Think about the final images that Lohrey frames them in. What have they learnt, if anything, from their experiences at Garra Nalla and the fire?

SETTING

Vertigo is set mainly on the coastline of Australia but there are references to the cityscape that they are escaping from. What we learn about setting is that the setting may allow healing and change but you cannot run away from yourself. Garra Nalla does supply some healing but it is the cathartic effect of the fire that is the biggest turning point. Before we analyse this we need to focus on the town itself which is a type of cumulative analysis by Lohrey of the Tasmanian towns that she has experienced, especially Falmouth, her own home town which did experience bushfires. These first hand experiences affected her own psyche and she explores this in the novella.

Garra Nalla is fictional but representational and is a cluster of eighty odd houses around a 'wild beach' and a lagoon and we can see the significance of that setting by Lohrey spending four pages (11–14) in describing it until we read,

> 'Perfect, they thought; *just perfect*.' (p14)

Another feature that Lohrey makes much of in the setting is the 'weatherboard homestead from the Federation era' which is also perfect for them as it was 'elemental'. Later we read that Luke becomes settled into this setting but Anna has some doubts about her ability to settle into the environment. Much of the discussion about setting has been handled in the sections on Distinctively Visual and in the techniques and so do not bear repeating here. Those sections give great detail on how the setting is used and how Lohrey invokes a variety of techniques to engage the reader and convey her ideas.

To conclude then I would just like to mention the 'Australianness' of *Vertigo* and its relationship to the country. Lohrey obviously has affection for the landscape and places of the Australian coastal setting. Despite the violence of the bushfire and the destruction it creates we still get a sense of affection for the natural landscape coming through in the writing and also for the wildlife that inhabits that environment. This is evident in Luke's birdwatching and the character's love of their town and its natural beauty.

The descriptions and events show a particular knowledge e.g. the use of casuarina's and the particular references to bird life of that environment. Lohrey creates a setting that we can all recognise but makes it different in an interesting manner and this is the reason that the novella has been so successful. It is a work about love but the love isn't just confined to characters, the setting makes it all happen and Lohrey's love of the natural landscape shines through in the character's experiences.

QUESTIONS ON THE SETTING

1. How does Lohrey portray the city? Do you think there might be some intentional bias on the part of the author? Explain your response with direct reference to *Vertigo*.

2. Why is Garra Nalla *'perfect'*?

3. What qualities does the old Federation house have that makes them choose it?

4. Discuss the lagoon. What impact does it have on the narrative?

5. How does the environment seem to enter the town and the characters manner of seeing the world? To respond to this question you could think about the wind and the descriptions of the wind, the tree line and the drought's impact.

6. How does the fire change the landscape? Note here it is not just the descriptions of the burnt areas but also the heat, smoke, dead animals and destroyed buildings. Comment on each of these.

7. What signs of regeneration/rebirth do we see at the end of the novella?

8. How do you think Lohrey conveys the idea that the setting we are in is constantly changing?

9. What images in your mind do the words 'seachange' and 'treechange' evoke? What are their actual meanings? These terms have come into our language over the last few decades as people move from the city for a more peaceful lifestyle. Research them and decide what kind of experience this might bring to families.

10. What makes this novella's setting particularly Australian?

CHARACTER ANALYSIS

Luke Worley

Luke is married to Anna and a through a major part of the narrative he is affected, as she is, by the problems arising from the death of their prematurely born son who is known as 'the boy'. At thirty-four Luke has taken to bird watching as a hobby, perhaps to alleviate the sense of loss. Dissatisfied with his life in the city he begins to feel that life is passing him by and that his optimism is fading 'into something jittery'. Anna agrees to his plan to move into the countryside, partly because she feels the same way. They eventually decide on the coastal hamlet of Garra Nalla where they find a Federation style house that suits them perfectly.

It is here Luke begins to change slowly finding something in the change that suits him. He becomes handy with things mechanical, a skill he hadn't had previously and slots into the more bucolic lifestyle easily. He is able to merge into the landscape of the town effectively and the surrounds, aided by his bird-watching. Luke begins to meld into the landscape as if he was a local and this doesn't always sit well with Anna who has plans to return to the city. It appears as if Luke will never do this as his brief trip back doesn't sit well with him. At a restaurant on the final night of his abbreviated stay,

> 'he is prickly and distant, complaining of the noise and making a show of not being able to hear anything said to him.' (p74)

'Nothing pleases him' and Anna is relieved when he goes. Anna and Luke have some issues and she sees him as 'complacent' and as having 'lost all ambition' yet Luke is unmoved and continues along without realising her concerns. He is lost in his commune with nature, the local life and the things and people that please him. Luke at the conclusion of the novella has come to terms with the loss of his child and we see this in the dream he has after the bushfire has passed and life has some semblance of normality,

> 'somewhere in there, lost to view, is the phantom of the bird on the banksia bough, and he sighs and groans in his sleep, for he'll never see that bird again, and he still doesn't know its name.' (p139)

Luke is a character that sees the visual around him and adapts clearly to his new environment. Certainly the bushfire clarifies and cleanses for him and the seachange that he undergoes affects more than his place of residence. The things he experiences change his personality and make him a different person.

Anna Worley

Anna has a different take on the seachange that she and Luke undergo and follows a different path into the reconciliation with her own life and the death of 'the boy'. While I feel she is reconciled with his death in the final section she struggles with other factors before coming to this moment when we leave the novella with her and the visually impactful 'ghostly images'. Anna has struggled with life after the death of her child (understandably) and the change she agrees to is partly to overcome this and change her life which she is generally unhappy with. We read this on page seven and eight,

'Anna appeared to put up little resistance to this migration and they assumed she was concerned about her health. What they couldn't know, because she didn't tell them, was that like her husband she found herself troubled by a falling away of her youthful elan.'

Anna doesn't fit into and adapt to the lifestyle at Narra Garra as easily as Luke who is more 'practical' than her but he understands her restlessness. She thinks that she couldn't 'live here all my life' but he ignores her and persists. Later in the novella she finds Luke a 'stranger' and feels,

> 'The world is spinning away from her. Something is dying, something is leaching away from them; some once vivid hue in the inner landscape of her consciousness is beginning to fade.' (p86)

Later, after the fire, she 'frets' for his return and when he does he has had his cathartic experience and cried for 'the boy' and they unite. That night she dreams of her lost child and wakes crying, showing her sensitivity to the issue. We see throughout *Vertigo* that she does begin to move on, even thinking about more children. Anna also seems to recover from her asthma to some extent and she certainly becomes more in tune with what is around her.

The Boy

The boy is a complex artifice in the novella and I would like you to think about his role in the novella and whether he can be considered a character as such. It is appropriate here to examine what Lohrey says about her creation,

'I don't want to say too much about him because I'll give away the plot, but he's another dimension of reality. You can read him in several ways. You can read him as a ghost, you can read him as a figment of their imagination. By the time you get to the end of the novella, as you know, you do realise who he is and why he is there. But one of the things I wanted to do was not write a wholly realistic story. I wanted to write a kind of fable, in a way, and so he sits in that as a fabulous figure who may or may not be real.

He relates directly to that sense of disorientation...when you move from the city to the country, as anyone who has made that move can tell you, you very often...all your expectations are confounded. The first thing you often experience is an intense disorientation, hence the title *Vertigo*, which does not relate to a fear of heights, by the way, but to the loss of balance that comes from being in a strange environment and having to find your bearings anew.

So there is this kind of element of the fable where there are certain magical or luminous elements that suggest a more powerful and mysterious reality, which is indeed really what nature is, a more powerful and mysterious reality, than the notion we have of it when we live in the city.'

http://www.abc.net.au/radionational/programs/bookshow/ amanda-lohreys-vertigo/3179466#transcript

Later in the questions I will ask what you think about this. Lohrey creates a kind of mystical/ ephemeral feel to 'the boy' and we can clearly see his impact on Luke and Anna. Certainly he is part of the book's experience for the audience but significantly he is important to the two main characters, Luke and Anna, who legitimately in their eyes see the boy as a living thing. He is upsetting the balance of their lives and they make decisions and have assumptions based on his life. This is challenged by the fire(s) and the move.

Gilbert Reilly

Gilbert 'Gil' Reilly is the closest neighbour in Garra Nalla and has a wonderfully extensive knowledge of 'local folklore' and he is fond of a 'natter'. His physical appearance is described,

> 'tall with a long beaky nose and ginger hair that is thin on top.' (p25)

Gil becomes a good friend and neighbour, helping them out with advice and practical assistance at times. He has his own family, four children, that don't visit but he doesn't live in the past and this is why Luke and Anna like him. Gil survives the bushfire and they come to think of him as part of why they like the move to the sea. Gil is practical and laconic in a typically Australian way, keeping his own business close and seeing the world with a wry, often ironic, humour. Gil is the kind of character one would expect to find in a small Australian town and in this regard he is nearly stereotypical yet the situation with the son gives him more depth.

The Watts Family

Alan and Bette Watts become friends with the Worley's and they socialise frequently despite the Watts having two children Briony and Zack. The Watts, 'belong to that coastal tribe who seem entirely at ease in their sun-ripened bodies and who rarely appear in anything other than shorts or thongs.' (p49)

The Watts are 'energetic and practical' and Luke and Anna seem to warm to them, even sharing confidences along with the barbecues. They have a terrible ordeal during the fire having to cling to the rocks in the bay and worrying about the children. We see Alan's priorities when he tells Luke the details of his 'dread' and Gil responds,

'It's all different when your kids are with you.'

The Watts form a counterpoint to the Worley's with their balanced family and easy acceptance of their way of life in Garra Nalla.

Questions on Character

1. Why does Luke want to leave the city and generate some new experiences? Is he thinking of himself or does he also have Anna in mind?

2. Analyse how Anna's life has changed in the time she has been married before the move to Garra Nalla. What experiences have changed her assumptions about life? Analyse her emotional state in response to these experiences as you read through the novella.

3. Discuss whether you think 'the boy' is a character and state reasons for your choice. What does he contribute to their experience of life and also your reading experience? i.e. did you find his presence confusing, irritating etc?

4. How does Luke change during his time in Garra Nalla? How do you see this change?

5. Describe how Anna comes to resent Luke's behaviour and lifestyle. Why are their experiences so different at this point of the novella? Do you think there may have been a middle ground to be found at this point?

6. What effect, if any, does Gil have on the couple? What experiences and human qualities does he bring to the community that encourage new ideas?

7. Would you say that Gil is an archetypal Australian country type of character or does he have a larger role than this in the novella?

8. Why might Lohrey include a character such as Rodney Banfield in *Vertigo*? Why might she need this contrast in the novella's mix? How does the community see Rodney? Does this collective opinion impact on how the newcomers see him?

9. Do you like the Watts family as characters? Analyse the reasons for your decisions about the family and include what role you think they play in *Vertigo*.

10. Discuss ONE other character not mentioned in this analysis and state what contribution they make to our understanding and appreciation of *Vertigo*.

THEMEMATIC CONCERNS

Human Experiences in *Vertigo*

Human experiences in the novella range from the very dramatic and emotive such as the death of Luke and Anna's child, the bushfire and the snake experience to the more mundane family issues such as personal disagreements and the relationship with the in-laws. The change in personal experiences for Luke and Anna can be seen early as they crave change because of the way their lives have shaped. They need new experiences to move forward in their lives and Luke says,

> 'He could feel his future coming towards him, indeed it was almost at his door, and it was not what he had hoped for.' (p5)

While Anna similarly feels,

> 'That most acidic of beasts, envy, had a fang-hold on her heart. She was past thirty, she was in a spiritual impasse and she needed to find a way out of it.' (p9)

To effect this change the couple decide to make it a whole new experience and move to a whole new environment to make this possible, intimating to us as an audience that sometimes a new experience involves not just personal change but a physical one as well. Here they can see a future,

> 'it was the reason they had chosen the place. They felt that in some essential way it was uncultivated, a landscape out of time, and as such it could not define them. Here they could live, and simply be.' (p14)

However Lohrey shows us you cannot leave all your experiences behind and the shadow of their child follows them from the city to their new home. He constantly reappears and if you are looking for concrete examples you can find him on pages 53, 123 and 134 for example and the whole story around his death and the hospital can be read on pages 130-1. Finally the boy is exorcised after the fire and the couple can move on.

Luke has wept finally for his loss . Amanda's response is,

> 'Ah,she says, so you are leaving us. So you are on your way at last. But it's okay, it's alright; yes, she thinks, I am ready for this, and she raises her arm in soft salute.' (p137)

This allows them to recover from the experiences of the past and rid themselves of the emotional baggage and assumptions that have so altered their way of seeing the world. Anna can now begin to think of the future and begin to plan,

> 'And she is thinking that she might go off the pill soon, that she is ready to try again. Life is so unpredictable: one cannot postpone decisions forever in the belief that things will be better down the track. What if, one day, there is no track?' (p137)

Part of this integration back into the world of positive experiences is the contributions of the local community. They are taught to canoe by one of the locals, they develop friendships in the community e.g. the Watts and also through the shared experiences they have with the bushfire and the near destruction of the town. These collective experiences have a bonding effect on people and develop commonalities of emotional experience as well as the physical and intellectual aspects. We can see this early when Gil welcomes them to the town,

> 'And Gil approves of the new settlers, the sea changers. 'They bring a bit of life to the district,' he says, 'and you can't expect things to stay the same.' (p26)

Gil is also there when she has her first encounter with a snake as she goes after the washing which has blown off the line. She is shaken by the incident as she had been 'so close' to it but as Gil points out,

> 'a copperhead. Your first snake. Now you can call yourself a local.' (p61)

These are the collective experiences that unite people and the snake is like a rite of passage. It is not just these dramatic experiences that Lohrey gives us in *Vertigo* but she also shows us the simpler personal characteristics that combine to give experiences. We see the interaction in the relationship between Luke and Anna and how they experience each other depending on the wants and moods of the other. Anna isn't as stoic as Luke and her emotional state is a moveable feast.

We see her mood impacted by such things as the wind,

> 'It's hard to describe the effect this weather has on my state of mind...I don't know if I can stand the drought much longer. I keep wondering if we've made a mistake.' (p62)

During the bushfire she is also upset,

> 'she says, crossly, for it is anger rather than fear that is going to carry her through this night.' (p119)

Luke is aware of her fluctuating state, something her father is incapable of. Luke knows,

'Luke Worley is not a fool. He can see that his wife is in need of a break. When friends in Randwick ring to say that they are about to travel overseas at short notice and ask if Luke and Anna would be interested in house-sitting, he feigns enthusiasm...' (p73)

Luke too has moments where he seems withdrawn or disinterested but they manage to use these experiences to overcome the serious issues in their lives.

So to recap we have seen that there are both collective and individual experiences in Vertigo that show how new ideas are developed and assumptions changed by coming to terms with old traumatic experiences and assumptions altered by experiencing new things – even on as harrowing as the bushfire – which are cathartic and renewing. Lohrey takes us through very personal experiences with her characters and shows how they respond emotionally and intellectually to these private experiences. We know from our reading that emotional responses are the strongest and this is where the power of the novella comes from. We will examine this more in the language section of this guide but first let's have a look at the imagery Lohrey incorporates.

THE VISUAL IMAGERY IN *VERTIGO*

We can think about the imagery in the novel in terms of how it conveys the human experience and this links integrally with the language section which follows. Firstly before a purely close analysis we should generally think about the idea of description in the novella. It is this description that builds images and pictures in the readers mind. This is how Lohrey conveys the narrative but also the emotions and thoughts of the characters. Later I shall discuss 'the boy' and how that picture, a very real picture, manifests itself in the minds of Luke and Anna. A description can be defined as 'a picture in words' and this is an excellent definition for our purpose because this is what Lohrey does for the first page when we read descriptions such as;

> 'There is too much urban jazz in the air, the drone of jets roaring in, the manic whine of sirens or the thumping bass line.' (p3)

Note here the use of sound to aid in the description. One aspect of good description is the use of the five senses to convey information. These senses (sight, sound, taste, touch and smell) are at the core of the novel's descriptions and help us build visual images of the people, places and events in the novel. Lohrey builds an image of dissatisfaction with the lives of her two main characters and we learn later that 'the boy' that is with them at times is a dead child that has scarred them both, but in different ways. The boy seems to choose when to appear, not much in the apartment but more when they are free. Lohrey deprives him as if he were real, as he is to Luke and Anna;

> 'Roused from his torpor on the back seat he craned his neck to see out, and wriggling free of his seatbelt

scrambled up onto the seat to press his face against the window.' (p11)

Lohrey even gives him personality, 'he remains loyal to his father' (81) and Anna can even touch and feel him;

> 'his open mouth sighs a warm breath and his eyelids flutter...With her finger she traces the rise of his high forehead, brushing aside the unruly whorls of fair hair...' (p123)

This is the power of an imaginative vision; his presence is distinctive and created by Lohrey to add depth to the characters and novel. Also consider the trauma of their loss and how it impacts how they see the world in general, does such a loss colour the world and those in it? Certainly an aspect to consider and another is the narrative line of Gil's 'the boy' who is fighting in Afghanistan. This narrative line with the boy is only one aspect of the imagery in the text and now I wish to explore how Lohrey creates imagery through language around the city and country.

It is too easy to state how this seeming paradox would be easy to write about with the bias that the city is bad and the township of Garra Nalla is perfect. Lohrey doesn't do this - she allows us to visualise the places she pictures and gives us an ambivalence that allows us to decide why the characters act as they do. The city causes Anna's asthma yet when she returns she is pleased to be out of the wind and;

> 'there is much here that is sensual and exciting, and not all of it neon. She loves the lurid metropolitan sunsets... the dark, blackish shapes of the city skyline, the contrast of their sharp-edged silhouettes against a fiery sky, confer on nature an even greater drama.' (p75)

Indeed we can see through these visualisations we can also see that Luke appreciates the country a little more initially and his bird watching integrated him into nature and the way of life there. Here Luke is happier, 'pointlessly, mindlessly happy' at times just by being in the natural world and a place where he seems to be content. They both find Garra Nalla a place of 'grandeur' and *just perfect* and the house their 'kingdom'. Examine these early descriptions carefully as they establish much that is relevant in the novel. Think about how you, as the audience, saw these places.

The other aspect of the narrative that deserves attention is the fire which dominates the final third of the book. Luke and Anna have had personal conflict and tension but the fire exacerbates this to an extent then draws them together, especially as the boy leaves. The intensity of the experience is described in detail and we see the emotional, as well as physical, impact it has on them and the community in general. Gil's relaxed,

> 'No-one dead,..so there you are.' (p128)

is typically Australian and unperturbed but for others it was traumatic because of the children. Yet it is the descriptions of the fire, beginning with smoke that attracts the attention of the reader. Lohrey's language engages us and draws us into the scene as if we are with them through the experience. As I have discussed earlier Lohrey had experienced fires herself and this experience is certainly translated into an understanding of the experience which is shared with us.

The fire itself begins with a 'brown smudge' and builds into,

> 'A yellow and red fireball is unravelling from the black underbelly of the smoke cloud. In one incandescent arc it

catapults high over the paddocks, across the freeway and down into the bush...' (p113)

To the aftermath of nothing but ash which upsets Luke so much,

'The wind funnelled anarchy of burning bush, the tidal wave of flame and smoke...'(p130)

The emotion drives him back to the waiting room where he learns of his son's death. The fire ignites emotion and then becomes cathartic. In many ways the fire mirrors their personal experience in that they needed the past to be cleansed away by fire so they can rise again.

Now I have briefly gone over what Lohrey does in the novella in the context of the imagery we next need to explore the specific techniques she uses to convey these images. I will do this in the next section on techniques.

Questions on Human Experiences

1. Define the term human experiences in your own words and apply this definition to *Vertigo*.

2. Name TWO images that contribute to the audiences understanding and enjoyment of the text and state what they contribute to the experience of one or more characters.

3. Discuss the difference between the city and the country as exposed in the novella. Do you think it is obvious or is Lohrey more subtle in differentiating character's experiences?

4. How do you define the term 'imaginative vision'?

5. Analyse the role of 'the boy' in *Vertigo* in terms of the human experience. Think about the way in which he contributes to

the emotions, ideas and assumptions different characters make.

6. Explain the role of the bushfire in the narrative. How does it enhance change? What types of conflict does it add to the narrative?

7. While we are focused on human experiences as our main idea we also need to think about other concepts that integrate into this idea. I think the novella is also about love, in its various forms. Do you agree with this thought? Explain your ideas with specific reference *Vertigo*.

8. Another thought that critics suggest Lohrey alludes to is that of the environment. Do you agree with this suggestion? Explain your response fully and then analyse what she is saying about the environment.

9. In a book that concentrates on the visual how does Lohrey convey emotions such as love?

10. Discuss ONE idea in *Vertigo* that hasn't been discussed here that YOU think is relevant to our understanding of the text in terms of understanding the human experience.

11. Do you consider *Vertigo* to be a good example of the representation of the human experience? Does it also offer something wider than this narrow view?

LANGUAGE

Language Techniques

In the previous section we have examined the manner in which Lohrey utilises the idea of human experiences in her novel and some of the ways in which she does this. Obviously description is one and I would like to give a specific example of the senses she writes into these descriptions. Let's look at one now with minor annotations,

> 'Concealed (sight) beneath a thicket of she-oaks they embraced (touch) on the spiky (touch) ground, enveloped in its pungent (smell) conifer scent and the sound (!) of the surf, it's soft wash (sound) against the rocks below.' (p43)

So it is easy to see how she uses the senses to develop a sense of place and allow us to 'see' that place which adds to the overall experience for the characters and the audience.

She also uses onomatopoeia to build images e.g. *'whoomph'* and similes such as 'burn like buggery' to communicate specific images through words. You should also note the use of italics throughout the novella as Lohrey uses them in interesting ways. She uses italics in the usual manner to highlight words for emphasis e.g. *'one'* (p41) and *'sure'* (p125) but also for Latin plant names, extracts from other literary works and titles. As well as these very specific language techniques that are used to compose highly visual images we need to examine some of the motifs that she uses to represent complex images.

'The boy' as their dead child is called is probably more than a recurring image in that he is so real to them and us he can be considered a character. He does of course represent their past experiences, a past they are trying to escape in their sea-change move. Eventually he goes, drifts away, with a wave on the water but I think that the motif that represents the boy as a character is the anonymous bird that Luke sees early. The bird is found dead after the fire and Luke is 'distraught' and Anna can't believe he is 'crazily upset about this...this one bird!' (p126) Luke also dreams of the phantom bird as a final sign that the boy has gone,

> 'And somewhere in there, lost to view, is the phantom of the bird on the banksia bough, and he sighs and groans in his sleep, for he'll never see that bird again, and he still doesn't know it's name.' (p139)

I have already covered much about 'the boy' in his character assessment so I will move into a discussion of another motif, that of the black swans. The black swans are, like the birds in the novella, transcendent of more mundane and mortal considerations. The black swans recur throughout and appear and disappear as they please. In the concluding sections the swans signify life returning to normalcy after the maelstrom of the fires,

> 'We haven't seen them since the fire...Their nesting grounds around the lagoon were burnt out and we wondered if they were dead, or flown away for good...the swans are back...' (p138)

USE OF PHOTOGRAPHS

Before we conclude this section it is vital to examine the use of the graphics in the novella. These are inserted into the text and form part of the visually distinctive effect that you need to fully understand the human experiences and how she shapes the representations of people and the reflections of personality. The quote below explains the use of the photos eloquently and Lohrey explains the purpose of their use,

> 'Some of the photographs she had. She had photographed the bushfires. So, for example, there's a marvellous photograph in the novella of a fireball. To my knowledge the only photograph of an actual fireball that's in existence, certainly the only one we've ever seen, and we've looked. A quite awe-inspiring image with a thrilling beauty to it.

So she already had some photographs, and then I told her about what I was doing, it was still in the draft stage, and the kinds of things I would like, that I would like some photographs of birds because birds feature quite strongly in the narrative. So she took some more photographs, and then I gave her the manuscript to read in draft and we sat down and we chose a long list of the ones we liked, and then we showed them to the publisher. So it was a kind of group effort. We came up with a small collection that we all liked.'

http://www.abc.net.au/radionational/programs/bookshow/ amanda-lohreys-vertigo/3179466#transcript

It is wise to comment on this aspect of the work in your essay and comment on why they were used and how they add meaning to your reading of *Vertigo*.

Questions on Techniques

1. Give TWO specific examples of human experiences and the techniques Lohrey uses to convey that image.

2. Why is important to create picture images in the readers mind in a novella such as *Vertigo*. Think about the short story format and the demands of that genre.

3. Find THREE descriptions that use at least four of the five senses. Why might an author such as Lohrey focus on using the senses to engage readers.

4. Comment on the use of one specific language technique used in *Vertigo* and analyse its effect in the novella.

5. Do you find 'the boy' more of a motif or a character? Explain your response with direct reference to *Vertigo*.

6. How do birds feature as motifs in Lohrey's work?

7. What particular importance does the unnamed bird have in the narrative?

8. Select ONE description of the bushfire and show, by annotation, how Lohrey creates a picture in the reader's mind.

9. Describe one image in the narrative that particularly struck you and why it impacted you.

10. Why has Lohrey combined with an artist to include graphics in the novella? What do they add to the narrative and the readers understanding?

11. If you had the opportunity to add a new graphic to *Vertigo*, what would it be and where in the novella would you place it.

THE ESSAY

The essay consists of the basic form of an introduction, body paragraphs and conclusion. The esssay has been the subject of numerous texts and you should have the basic form well in hand. As teachers, the point we would emphasise would be to link the paragraphs both to each other and back to your argument (which should directly respond to the question). Of course, ensure your argument is logical and sustained.

Make sure you use specific examples and that your quotes are accurate. To ensure that you respond to the question, make sure you plan carefully and are sure what relevant point each paragraph is making. It is solid technique to actually 'tie up' each point by explicitly coming back to the question.

When composing an essay the basic conventions of the form are:

- State your argument, outline the points to be addressed and perhaps have a brief definition.

A solid structure for each paragraph is:
- Topic sentence (*the main idea and its link to the previous paragraph/ argument*)
- Explanation/ discussion of the point including links between texts if applicable.
- Detailed evidence (*Close textual reference – quotes, incidents and technique discussion.*)
- Tie up by restating the point's relevance to argument/ question

- Summary of points
- Final sentence that restates your argument

As well as this basic structure, you will need to focus on:

Audience – for the essay the audience must be considered formal unless specifically stated otherwise. Therefore, your language must reflect the audience. This gives you the opportunity to use the jargon and vocabulary that you have learnt in English. For the audience ensure your introduction is clear and has impact. Avoid slang or colloquial language including contractions (like 'doesn't', 'e.g.', 'etc.').

Purpose – the purpose of the essay is to answer the question given. The examiner evaluates how well you can make an argument and understand the module's issues and its text(s). An essay is solidly structured so its composer can analyse ideas. This is where you earn marks. It does not retell the story or state the obvious.

Communication – Take a few minutes to plan the essay. If you rush into your answer it is almost certain you will not make the most of the brief 40 minutes to show all you know about the question. More likely you will include irrelevant details that do not gain you marks but waste your precious time. Remember an essay is formal so **do not** do the following: story-tell, list and number points, misquote, use slang or colloquial language, be vague, use non-sentences or fail to address the question.

PLAN:

Don't even think about starting without one!

Introduce... the texts you are using in the response *Argument*: The human experience is affected by: ▪ Idea One ▪ Idea Two ▪ Idea Three	You need to let the marker know what texts you are discussing. You can start with a definition but it can come in the first paragraph of the body. You MUST state your argument in response to the question and the points you will cover as part of it. Wait until the end of the response to give it!

Idea One – Aspect of human experience as outlined in the textual material, e.g. physical impact. **Idea Two –** Another aspect of human experience as outlined in the textual material, e.g. psychological impact. ▪ explain the idea ▪ where and how is it shown in the prescribed text? ▪ where and how is it shown in related text 1? **Idea Three** – People's sense of experience is affected by context and environment ▪ explain the idea ▪ where and how shown in the prescribed text? ▪ where and how shown in related text 1?	You can use the things you have learned to organise the essay. For each one, you say where you saw this in your prescribed text and where in related text(s). Two or three ideas are usually enough as you can explore them in detail.

▪ Summary of two key ideas ▪ Final sentence that restates your argument	Make sure your conclusion restates your argument. It does not have to be too long.

MODEL ESSAY OUTLINE

> **To what extent are human experiences significant in the set text?**
>
> **From your studies respond to this question using your set text and at ONE piece of other textual material**

This essay needs to be attacked in a manner that responds to the question and shows ALL your knowledge about the text. The question lends itself to a close study of Amanda Lohrey's *Vertigo* as the text does show how the human experience is integral to life and how it shapes our other experiences and interaction with the world.

An introduction might be written:

> Human experiences are important in Lohrey's novel *Vertigo* and the two related texts Lawrence's film *Jindabyne* and Ed Sheeran's song *Castle on the Hill*. These texts show how human experiences are integral to human existence and bring more meaning to one's life. Life is about experiences that challenge us and define how we see the world. They shape our beliefs and attitudes and can be confronting at the same time. Without experiences our lives would be empty and meaningless.

Your essay should then follow the outlined plan and develop these ideas. This gives you the opportunity to link the texts and fully develop each of the ideas.

ANNOTATED RELATED MATERIAL:
DIFFERENT STUDIES OF HUMAN EXPERIENCES

Jindabyne – Ray Lawrence

Jindabyne is an Australian film that captures a wide array of human experiences. It touches on the ideas mentioned in the introduction to this text in a number of detailed instances. We can begin by considering the following before beginning a detailed examination of the narrative.

The collective human experience:

- Aboriginality and the spiritual;
- The Fishermen and their code;
- The reaction of the townsfolk;
- Media response;
- Interaction with the natural world.

Individual Experience:

- An individual character's response to the body – choose one;
- The killer;
- Response to the revelations;
- Past experiences and how they impact on current experiences;
- Reaction to loss – emotional;
- Assumptions about life.

We can now look at the plot to help us understand each of these issues. *Jindabyne* begins with the sound of a radio being tuned and the Australian feel of the movie is immediate with the theme music for the ABC news. Lawrence emphasises the isolation by having the radio not tune in correctly for an unknown female character, forcing her to use the cassette player. With this unusual beginning we know that her experience is not going to be positive.

We then pan to the rocks slowly where Gregory, our killer, sits patiently in a truck with the engine running watching the road. We know he is prepared for this as he has binoculars. He sees an Aboriginal girl, Susan O'Connor, driving and she is the one fiddling with the radio. He chases her down and forces her to stop. He moves toward her as we see a long shot of how isolated they are. We see his face in her window looming above her and screaming about the electricity coming down from the mountains. This film is no murder mystery, as we know from the beginning that the murderer is Gregory the electrician. This is about the experiences of the other characters in the film and how they respond to current experiences.

The Kane family, Stewart, Claire and son Tom, is waking. Claire pretends to sleep, before waking suddenly and being affectionate with Tom. Stewart and Tom head out fishing. The scene doesn't feel quite right and there is some emotional tension between Stewart and Claire that is unspoken due to what they have experienced in the past. Claire had a complicated past when she was pregnant with Tom. When she finds she is pregnant again, she becomes emotional and slightly unstable.

As the film builds we see the complex pasts of the characters and their interactions in the confinement of the small town. The fishing trip is a break from this and extremely important in their lives.

We see some of the emotional instability in characters such as Caylin-Calandria, who with Tom, has some issues at school. Along with Caylin-Calandria, Claire and Jude also have issues but in a nicely framed shot of the three female characters, we see them conform as members of a close knit group. The sacrifice they make is similar to Gregory's but on a different scale. Note the connection here and how each one is to get back to order and societal norms. This is the collective experience for all the characters.

At the Kanes' home the tensions are obvious from their past experiences but they contain it for appearances' sake. Occasionally, the tension reaches breaking point and the experience strains the superficial approach. The tension builds at home and the fishing trip seems like a good opportunity to break the cycle.

When we see Gregory dump Susan O'Connor's body in the river, we know that the fishing and her death will interact.

The next morning, the fishermen head off for their one big trip of the year and the sign 'Gone fishing' is put in the garage window. We see Billy on the phone to Elissa and putting the sign the wrong way round in the window shows his immaturity. They have already said they are taking him away to make a man of him. The four men have a few beers on the way and talk as they travel through the landscape. They intend to give Billy the experience they think he needs as a 'man' — a cultural rite of passage.

The men arrive and the high-tension electricity wires punctuate the wilderness. They begin to hike toward the valley. It's a long walk in and the terrain is hilly and difficult. They stop on the way and again we see Billy's naivety when Stewart says 'Listen to that' meaning the silence but he can't, as he has his earphones in. It is part of the break in tension of the film that they commune with nature. This experiential break affects all the men. The episode represents a distinct human experience.

Stewart wanders down the river fishing and sees Susan's body caught in the rocks. Hesitantly, he wades out to it and turns it over saying 'Oh Jesus' repeatedly. He screams for the others to come as he drags the body to the bank. He is obviously upset, making the sign of the cross. Stewart tells Rocco to 'take her, for fuck's sake, take her' and their shock is obvious. They all stare at the body and Billy goes to run off but they stop him. The four men meet and decide to leave her in the water and tie her so she doesn't float away.

The presence of the body threatens to detract from the enjoyment of the fishing experience. The act of attempted isolation of the bad experience is expected to evoke only a mild response. They do not anticipate the stormy reaction it receives when they return to the community.

The men go on fishing, with Stewart getting the first big fish on an absolutely perfect day. The lure of the fish is strong, especially when they see the big one he has caught. They have a successful and enjoyable time, a positive experience. They get a photo of the catch and Billy holds up his fish in a typical hunter/gatherer pose. Capturing an experience this way is most enjoyable.

It is a photo that will come back to haunt them as things change back in the world. An unanticipated adverse reaction can be a horrific experience.

Stewart goes to check on the dead girl, rolling her over and getting debris off her face in a quite tender gesture. The next day they head back and report it. At the car Billy rings Elissa and says they found a body but 'caught the most amazing fish'. They are told by the police to wait and seem despondent their trip has been ruined. They organise their story as Stewart says they have 'to get their story straight'.

We cut to Gregory eating breakfast and he appears to be a normal, lonely man until he goes out to his shed where he has hidden Susan's car and this reminds us of the evil in him. Consider his experience and his motivations. How does he see his actions and the world?

The next day at the station the policeman tells the fishermen 'we don't step over bodies for our recreational pursuits' and 'the whole town's ashamed of you'. When they are told to 'piss off' from the station the press are waiting for them and Billy makes a comment. Carl is angry with the press but we can begin to see signs of distress within the whole group.

The experience they had so looked forward to has become a negative one and the tensions we saw before are exacerbated by the emotional and collective response to the murder. Claire soon becomes obsessed with the whole affair because of her own state. The newspaper the next day has the headline, 'Men fish over dead body' because Billy has talked. Billy is late to work and Stewart tells him they have to 'stick together on this'.

Susan's sister calls them 'animals' and raises the race question by asking if they would have left a white girl. The Aboriginal youths begin to attack and vandalise the property of the men in violent outbursts, including throwing a rock through Billy's van window and thus endangering his baby. They insult Carl at the caravan park and vandalise the garage.

The police aren't any help and the situation deteriorates. Jude tells the police they shouldn't be enforcing the 'political correctness' laws. The intervention of the sense of Aboriginality and race challenges the assumptions people have and how we see the world. The contrasting views are ingrained in the social structures and part of different collective experiences.

The Aboriginal people see the white people as 'interfering' and the group of fishermen begin to fight amongst themselves. Elissa says they shouldn't go to the bush at all as it's sacred. The group talk about the bush and Rocco punches Stewart for saying the Aborigines are superstitious. The experience of racial tension becomes ever-present and adds to the emotional responses to the experience.

We now head slowly to a resolution of the conflict brought about by the various experiences. Each is handled in a different manner by characters and you can explore one or two of the responses. To cycle back to the original murder, Claire is stalked by Gregory in his truck. He stops her but drives off after staring weirdly, an odd experience in itself.

Terry and Stewart talk and Stewart meets Rocco and Carl. He tells them Claire's left him 'again'. Rocco can't believe it and we cross cut to her looking out into the wilderness after he looks thoughtfully out the window. These different reactions to experiences mirror attitudes in life and reactions to emotional and intellectual conflict.

In conclusion, Lawrence takes us back to the healing power of nature in our human experiences when the Aboriginal people are having a ceremony. Gregory watches while Claire walks in. Again we see his truck as an omnipresent force in the film, almost an extension of him. An Aboriginal man tells Claire to 'piss off' from the ceremony after she says she has come to pay her 'respects' but he is told to leave her alone by an Auntie.

The smoke and tribal music symbolise the ceremonial nature of the setting and the camera pans around the scene and the bush. We see parts of the ceremony with chanting and clapping sticks. The camera moves in and out while other shots pan around the bush, giving us the full experience and Lawrence portrays this as a positive, healing experience.

Eventually Stewart, Tom, Carl, Jude and Rocco arrive to pay respects. Tom runs to his mother and Stewart goes over and says 'Sorry' but is rebuffed by the father who throws dirt on him and spits, refusing his apology. Then an Aboriginal girl tells a little about Susan's story and sings the last love song Susan wrote.

The camera pans around all the faces as they listen to the song and the ceremonial smoke wafts around. It seems to have some healing effect on everyone, as it is a meaningful experience which raises the idea of the spiritual experience in the text. The girl stops singing through emotion. 'Be gone' seems to symbolise in language the whole scenario for each character.

We see a long wide shot of the bush before fading back to Gregory waiting again in his car behind the rocks for another victim. It is quite a circular conclusion and it is an odd end when he crushes the fly. We don't quite know what to make of the whole experience and he seems to be the only character unchanged by the experiences in the film.

Poem: 'Inland' by John Kinsella

The poem captures the mood and ethos of the outback farming communities and deals with the human aspect more than some of the other poems in Kinsella's collection: *Peripheral Light*. This poem is one long restless thought that mimics memories and recollection while raising the current, topical issues that concern the poet. As usual with his poems Kinsella orientates the audience early with the word 'Inland' and then continues the poem without a full stop. The poem flows with the use of commas but Kinsella allows us to stop and think with the use of the colon, brackets and the hyphen. Look for these punctuation stops as you read as they emphasise a specific point or idea that resonates with the audience.

The first stanza gives us a foreshadowing of the events to follow with the warnings in the words 'storm', 'alert' and 'uncertain'. This ominous tone is reinforced by the word 'ghosts' and the implication of death which is constant in much of Kinsella's poetry. The next stanza deals with a more human element and we get the country feel with the bracketed gossip about McHenry's accident which shows the close knit community. Habits here are formed as part of survival and known to all as we see 'the old man plying the same track' and the families possibly heading to church on the Sunday morning.

The third stanza returns to the vagaries of nature. Kinsella repeats 'uncertain' with regard to the weather. Weather and the environment play a large role in farming communities and it is especially so at sowing and harvest. Despite the uncertainty and 'ashen' days which alter 'moods', the community returns to their habits and routines which shape their lives. The next stage returns to the road and the implication of a journey but a journey that is straight and in conflict with the cycles of the natural world. The path seems already marked and measured. It is 'straight and narrow', marked by a theodolite.

The final four lines of the poem are pure Kinsella, marking the transience of humanity on the landscape. We read

> 'it's a place of borrowed dreams
> where the marks of the spirit
> have been erased by dust –
> the restless topsoil'

The European farmers had 'borrowed dreams' for their own relationship with the land but this line also harks back to the indigenous Dreamtime when the land was created. The indigenous view that the land owns the people is also true for Kinsella. This sense of nobody owning the land is strong in his poetry. European impact on the land can be seen in the spirituality being removed by the dust—dust created by the poor farming techniques transferred from a different land. He finishes with the 'restless topsoil' as if the whole earth is moving in its own discontented journey, just as the people move.

The influence here of genuinely lost spirituality and connection with the land as we move directly on the 'high road' contrasts with the more flowing, 'restless' side of the natural world. This visual contrast is obvious but we can also discuss the contrast between habit and spirit. 'Inland' is a poem that uses the landscape to show the contrast between two views of the countryside.

DRAMA: Eugene O'Neil's *Desire Under the Elms*

O'Neill sets out to instruct how the house and elms should appear and the year is 1850. Note how he describes the 'enormous' elms as,

> 'exhausted women resting their sagging breasts and hands and hair on its roof, and when it rains their tears trickle down monotonously and rot on the shingles'

and how they dominate and 'rot'. It is important to read this both in terms of the play and in the context of American theatre. The description here shows O'Neill's genius at new design and original theatricality.

Part One: Scene One

The whole first page and a third are nearly all playwright notes that describe the farm, the house and the characters of Eben, Simeon and Peter. The first words of the play, 'God! Purty!' reflect the beauty of the land and how Eben perceives it. Eben is 'resentful and defensive' and feels 'trapped' on the farm.

His older half-brothers Simeon and Peter are 'more bounce and homelier in face, shrewder and more practical.' They all have worked hard on their father's farm over the years and have little feeling for their absent father. We learn that Simeon had a 'woman' who died and that Peter is excited by the prospect of 'gold in the West'. They all talk about how hard they've worked and hope that the father might 'die soon'. What we get from all this is that they are earthy and this is reflected in their bodies and clothes which are all dirt stained.

We also see here the difference between them as Eben sees gold in the pasture, not California, as they head in for a dinner of bacon in what seems a ritual they have performed many times before. Note that O'Neill calls for the use of the curtain at the end of the scene.

Scene Two

It is twilight and again we get detailed notes on the interior scene. Simeon tells Eben he should not wish their father dead and Eben replies he's not his son but, 'I'm Maw – every drop of blood!' He then blames the father, Ephraim Cabot, for killing his mother by working her to death but the others just say there was work to be done. O'Neill gets them to list the jobs and Eben comes back with 'vengeful passion' that, while they did nothing, he will see his mother gets 'rest and sleep in her grave!'

They then discuss Cabot's absence and how he just drove off in a buggy one day in a rush. Simeon says that when he went,

> 'He druv off in the buggy, all spick an' span, with the mare all breshed an' shiny, druv off clackin' his tongue an' wavin' his whip. I remember it quite well'

Eben mocks Simeon for not stopping him and the scene concludes with Eben leaving to see Minnie the town whore. We learn all the Cabot men have slept with her. Simeon and Peter say that Eben is just like 'Paw' and thinks of California. The final image is of Eben with his arms stretched to the sky talking about starts and sin, 'my sin's as purty as any one on 'em!', until he 'strides' to the village for Min.

Scene Three

It is 'pitch darkness' and Eben comes home with the news that Cabot has married a 'purty' thirty-five year old. He has heard this in the village and this effectively disinherits the boys. Simeon and Peter see California as their only option now. Eben tells the boys that they can have three hundred dollars each if they sign their share of the farm over to him. He can get the money as his mother told him,

> 'I know whar it's hid. I been waitin' – Maw told me. She
> knew whar it lay fur years, but she was waitin'....It's her'n
> – the money he hoarded from her farm an' hid from Maw.
> It's my money by rights now.'

They think about it and Eben tells them about his night with Min. He tells how he hates the new wife after the boys suggest he might sleep with her, just like Min, to get the old man back. Peter and Simeon say they'll do the deal and leave the farm. Both are bitter and vindictive about Cabot.

Scene Four

The setting is the same as Scene Two and the boys are discussing how they don't have to work now – it is all down to Eben who is jubilant as he thinks it will all be his. Peter and Simeon again reflect on how like his father he is, 'Like his Paw'. They also tell he isn't much of a milker but they soon talk about their leaving and how they'll miss some aspects of the farm.

Eben comes back in and says that the 'old mule an the bride' are coming. The two older boys begin to pack and sign Eben's papers as he gives them the money Cabot had hidden. They tell him they'll send him 'a lump o' gold for Christmas' and head into the yard feeling 'light' because of their newfound freedom.

Ephraim Cabot and Abbie Putnam then come in and O'Neill describes them in detail. Cabot is

> 'seventy-five, tall and gaunt, with great, wiry, concentrated power, but stoop shouldered by toil. His face is hard as if it were hewn from a boulder, yet there is a weakness in it'

but his face is weakened with petty pride. Abbie is

> 'thirty-five, buxom, full of vitality. Her round face is pretty but marred by its rather gross sensuality. There is strength and obstinacy in her jaw, a hard determination in her eyes, and about her whole personality.'

She also has a 'desperate quality'. Cabot shows Abbie the place and she says to him it's 'mine'. Then he sees the two boys not working. He introduces Abbie and she goes to look at 'her' house and they warn her Eben's inside.

Cabot tells them to get to work and they give him cheek, saying they are 'free' and heading to California. They 'whoop' it up and he says he'll have them chained up. They throw rocks at the house, smashing the window and head off singing. Abbie sticks her head out the window and says she likes the room but he is thinking of the stock and 'almost runs' to the barn.

Abbie then meets Eben in the kitchen and talks to him in 'seductive tones'. She says she doesn't want to be his 'Maw' but friends and he cusses her. She tells him of her troubled life and how Cabot gave her a chance to escape it. He calls her a 'harlot' and they argue over ownership of the farm. She has the upper hand in law and he leaves but the seeds of their growing attraction have been set.

Outside he and his father argue about life and work and he tells Eben 'Ye'll never be more'n half a man!' The scene ends with Abbie washing up and the faint notes of the song the boys were singing as they left.

Part Two: Scene One

Again O'Neill describes in detail the farmhouse setting. Two months have passed and it is a hot Sunday afternoon. Abbie in her best outfit is sitting on the porch and Eben comes out of the house also dressed in his best. They stalk each other, both attracted and repelled. As he walks away she 'gives a sneering, taunting chuckle' at him and they argue but the attraction is obvious. She says that nature will pull him to her but he says that she is married and he goes to leave her.

She accuses him of going to Min and she gets angry stating he'll never get the farm,

> 'Ye'll never live t' see the day when even a stinkin' weed on
> it 'll belong t' ye!'

He says he hates her and leaves as Cabot enters. She tells him Eben has been mocking him and twists the conversation to the inheritance of the farm. She tells him Eben lusts after her and as he angers she backs off in her accusations. Reassured, he says that she can have the farm if she bears the son she says she wants with him. He says that he'd 'do anythin' ye axed, I tell ye!' if she gave him a son and tells her to pray to God for it to happen.

Scene Two

It is about eight in the evening and here the bedrooms are highlighted, with Eben in one and Cabot with Abbie in the other. The two of them are talking about a son. They seem together, yet apart, as he tells her of his life on the farm and how God's hard. He both lost and gained on the way through, but the farm is his. He says he is pleased he found her, his 'Rose o' Sharon'. Abbie promises him that she will bear a son as he basically threatens her,

> 'Ye don't know nothin' – nor never will. If ye don't hev a son t' redeem ye...'

and he leaves to sleep in the barn with the cows 'whar it's restful'.

We then see Eben and Abbie restless and she leaves the room and goes to him. He 'submits' to her kisses then 'hurls' her away. Abbie says she'd make him 'happy' and she knows he wants her too much. She tells him to go down to the parlour and he is shocked as this is where his mother was 'laid out'. She leaves for the parlour and he wonders what's happening. The scene closes with a question to his dead mother, 'Maw! Whar are yew?' but we know that he wants her and will go to her.

Scene Three

The scene now shifts to the parlour which is described as a 'grim, repressed room like a tomb'. Abbie waits and Eben appears and he sits at her invitation. They talk about his Maw and how they hate Cabot. Abbie throws herself at him with 'wild passion' and he is caught up in the moment and thinks that it's his Maw wanting him to sleep with Abbie to get revenge on Cabot,

I see it! I sees why. It's her vengeance on him – so's she
kin rest quiet in her grave!

Abbie proclaims her love for him and he for her then they kiss 'in
a fierce, bruising kiss' to close the scene.

Scene Four

A more bold and confident Eben leaves the house and Abbie opens
the parlour window. She calls him over for a kiss and they talk a
bit before Eben says his Maw can now rest. They split as Cabot
comes out of the barn but are now obviously in love. Eben tells
Cabot that his Maw is now at rest and Cabot says he rests best
with the cows. Cabot is confused but the scene ends with him
criticising Eben as 'Soft-headed' and a 'born fool' but, being a
practical man, he heads for breakfast.

Part Three: Scene One

Time has passed to 'late spring the following year'. Eben is upstairs
in emotional and psychological conflict while a party happens
downstairs. Cabot has drunk too much and Abbie sits, pale and
thin, in a rocking chair. There is a fiddler and Abbie begins the
scene by asking for Eben and the guests 'titter' as most think the
baby is Eben's, not Cabot's, which is true enough. They laugh and
Cabot is angered by this and orders them to dance. The fiddler
'slyly' says they're waiting for Eben but Cabot mocks the boy and
then ensues a bawdy conversation about his fertility,

I got a lot in me – a hell of a lot – folks don't know on.
Fiddle 'er up, durn ye! Give 'em somethin' t' dance t!'

The fiddler plays and they dance. Cabot joins in frantically and 'whoop(s)' it up. He exhausts the fiddler and pours whiskey. In the upstairs room Eben is looking at the baby. Abbie goes upstairs and Cabot leaves for outside, 'fresh air', as she has told him not to 'tech' her. The guests gossip after he goes and we see Eben and Abbie upstairs and she professes her love for him,

'Don't git feelin' low. I love ye, Eben. Kiss me.'

Cabot says he's going to rest in the barn. The scene concludes with the fiddler playing in celebration of 'the old skunk gittin' fooled!'

Scene Two

Eben is outside half an hour later and Cabot is coming back from the barn. Cabot tells him to get a woman inside and he might get a farm. Eben replies that this farm's his and Cabot mocks him. He tells her Abbie has been promised the farm for her son and Eben is angered thinking Abbie has tricked him.

Eben goes to kill her but Cabot is too strong for him and Abbie comes out to stop him choking Eben. Cabot tells him he's weak and goes inside to celebrate. Abbie tries to be tender with Eben but he rejects her and calls her a liar.

'Ye're nothin' but a stinkin' passel o' lies. Ye've been lyin' t' me every word ye spoke, day an' night, since we fust – done it. Ye've kept sayin' ye loved me....'

She says she loves him and tells him that the promise was made before they fell in love. He says he'll go to California.

They argue and he 'torturedly' says he wished the baby had never been born. Abbie is distraught and she says she'd kill the baby to prove her love for him. He says he won't listen to her but she calls after him that she can 'prove' she loves him and she 'kin do one thin' God does'. Abbie is desperate at the end of the scene.

Scene Three

It is now just before dawn and Eben is in the kitchen ready to leave. Abbie is near the cradle with 'her face full of terror'. She sobs but Cabot stirs and she goes to the kitchen and flings her arms around Eben, kissing him 'wildly'. She says 'I killed him' and he thinks she means Cabot but is horrified when she tells him it's the baby.

Eben states it was his baby and she says she loved it but loves him more. He is angered,

> 'Don't ye tech me! Ye're pizzen! How could ye – t' murder a pore little critter – Ye must've swapped yer soul t' hell!

and tells her that he is getting the Sheriff and heads, 'panting and sobbing' to town. She calls out to him that she loves him.

Scene Four

It is after dawn and Abbie is in the kitchen. Cabot wakes in his room and is concerned that he has woken late. He checks the baby and is proud it is quiet and asleep. He goes down to Abbie in the kitchen and she tells him the baby is dead. He runs to check and comes back down and asks 'why?'

In a rage she tells him it was Eben's son and that she loves Eben, not him. He blinks back a tear and then gets 'stony' so he can carry on and says he is going to get the Sheriff. Abbie tells him that Eben's already gone so that Cabot tells her he'll 'git t' wuk.' He then tells her he'd never have told and now he's going to be 'lonesomer'n ever!' Eben comes back and Cabot tells him to get off the farm.

Eben asks for her forgiveness and tells her he loves her. He says he realised he loved her at the Sheriff's and they have a chance to run away but Abbie says she'll take her punishment. Eben says he will share it with her and plans to tell the Sheriff they planned it together. They think they can stand it together and then Cabot comes back.

He goes into a long tirade and tells them how he's let the stock go and will burn the house down. He too plans to go to California but finds that Eben has gotten to his money first. Cabot says that this is a sign from God to him to stay and that 'God's hard an' lonesome!' At this point the Sheriff comes and Eben says he was involved with the baby's murder.

Cabot says 'Take 'em both' and leaves to get his stock. The sun is coming up and as they are led away Eben says the farm's 'Purty' and Abbie agrees. The Sheriff finishes the play with the line, 'It's a jim-dandy farm, no denyin'. Wish I owned it!'

OTHER RELATED TEXTS

Fiction / Non-fiction / Drama

- *Wonder* – R G Palacio
- *First they Killed My Father* – Luong Ung
- *The Graveyard Book* – Neil Gaiman
- *Looking for Alaska* – John Green
- *Eleanor and Park* by Rainbow Rowell
- *The Fault in Our Stars* – John Green
- *We All Fall Down* – Robert Cormier
- *The Old Man and the Sea* – Ernest Hemingway
- *The Fire Eaters* – David Almond
- *Ender's Game* – Orson Scott Card
- *Hatchet* – Gary Paulsen
- *Inside Black Australia* – Kevin Gilbert
- *Sapiens: A Brief History of Humankind* – Yuval Noah Harari
- *Peeling the Onion* – Wendy Orr
- *Raw* – Scott Monk
- *Six Degrees of Separation* – John Guare
- *The Book Thief* – Markus Zusak
- *When Dogs Cry* – Markus Zusak
- *Holes* – Louis Sachar
- *The Outsiders* – S.E. Hinton
- *Roll of Thunder, Hear My Cry* – Mildred D. Taylor
- *A Small Free Kiss in the Dark* – Glenda Millard
- *Monster* – Walter Dean Myers
- *Lord of the Flies* – William Golding
- *Jandamarra* – Steve Hawke
- *A Separate Peace* – John Knowles
- *A Monster Calls* – Patrick Ness
- *The Pigman* – Paul Zindel
- *The Invention of Hugo Cabret* – Brian Selznik

- *Emerald City* – David Williamson
- *Silent Spring* – Rachel Carson

Films and Television

- *The Human Experience* – Charles Kinnane
- *My Brilliant Career* – Gillian Armstrong
- *Broadchurch* – James Strong & Euros Lyn
- *Twinsters* – Samantha Futerman and Ryan Miyamoto
- *Be My Brother* – Genevieve Clay - Smith
- *What's Eating Gilbert Grape* – Lasse Hallstrom
- *Pleasantville* – Gary Ross
- *Eternal Sunshine of the Spotless Mind* – Michel Gondry
- *Taxi Driver* – Martin Scorsese
- *Tootsie* – Sydney Pollack
- *Back in Time for Dinner* – Kim Maddever
- *The Godfather* – Francis Ford Coppola
- *Friends* – David Crane and Marta Kaufmann
- *Dawson's Creek* – Kevin Williamson
- *Orange is the New Black* – Jenji Kohan
- *Boy Meets World* – Michael Jacobs and April Kelly

Website – quote on literature and the human experience

*http://view2.fdu.edu/academics/university-college/school-of-humanities/
english-language-and-literature-program/*

> At its most fundamental level literature explores what it means to be a human being in this world and tries to describe what our human experience is like. As such, literature pushes us to confront the large human questions that have plagued humankind for centuries: issues of fate and free will, issues relating to our role in the universe, our relationship to God, and our

relationships with others. Studying literature not only helps us to understand the complexity of these questions intellectually, but because of its very nature, it allows us to experience these tensions vicariously. Literature does not just tell us about human experience; it recreates it in a way we can feel and visualise. In other words, it calls for a total response from us—it stretches us beyond who we are.

First, literature can enhance our ability to relate to people. Because literature focuses on human relationships and self perception, it can broaden our own experience—to help us understand different kinds of people, different cultures, different problems—and, consequently, help us better understand our own relationships with others.

The study of literature also helps to foster an appreciation for beauty, symmetry, and order. This means more than the intuitive response of liking or disliking something we see or read or hear; it means a carefully thought-through response that will enhance appreciation—not destroy it.

Perhaps the most important skills that the study of literature teaches are analytic and synthetic skills. In learning to read carefully and analytically, we learn to ask hard questions both of the work and of ourselves. And as we seek to discover the relationships between the ideas and images we uncover in a work, our ultimate goal is to see the whole—to see how the parts work together to make the piece what it is. In grappling with the complex and difficult ideas contained in literature, we learn to accept the multiple dimensions and ambiguity that are so often present in life.

Finally, the study of literature will also help develop our writing abilities as we come to value the written word and understand its power to communicate.

Beyond all of these skills, however, it is not what literature can do for us as individuals as much as what it can do to us. Literature speaks to the whole person. Listen to it, says C. S. Lewis, and you will be changed.

Poetry

- 'Warren Pryor' – Alden Nowlan
- 'The Gardener' – Louis MacNeice
- 'The Improvers' – Colin Thiele

Songs

- *Be My Escape* – Relient K
- *Mandolin Wind* – Rod Stewart
- *Roxanne* – The Police
- *Wake Me Up When September Ends* – Green Day
- *Under Pressure* – Queen & David Bowie
- *Candle in the Wind* – Elton John
- *Empire State of Mind* – Alicia Keys
- *Gold Digger* – Kanye West
- *We Are Young* – Fun.
- *Centrefold* – J. Geils Band
- *It's Time* – Imagine Dragons
- *We Cry* – The Script
- *If I Were a Boy* – Beyoncé
- *Shake it Out* – Florence + the Machine
- *C'mon* – Panic! At the Disco & Fun.
- *I Don't Love You* – My Chemical Romance
- *Sing* – My Chemical Romance
- *1985* – Bowling for Soup
- *What About Me* – Shannon Noll
- *Sinner* – Jeremy Loops
- *7 Years* – Lucas Graham

- *Bitter Sweet Symphony* – The Verve
- *Ghost!* – Kid Kudi
- *Good Riddance (Time of Your Life)* – Green Day
- *Expectations* – Belle and Sebastian
- *After Hours* – We Are Scientists
- *Write About Love* – Belle and Sebastian
- *Trust Your Stomach* – Marching Band
- *Heaven Knows I'm Miserable Now* – The Smiths